OPTIONS PROFITS USING DECISION CHARTS

Dr. Jon Schiller

OPTIONS PROFITS USING DECISION CHARTS

Aggressive Strategies
for the Most Lucrative Options Markets

including
OEX Index Options
QLD/QID Autotrade
SPY, QQQQ
16 High Performance Stocks Options
17 High Profit Potential Futures Options

Jon Schiller, PhD

BOOKSURGE
CHARLESTON, SC

2008

Now Published by BOOKSURGE
Charleston, SC 29418
Printed in the United States of America

First Published By Jon Schiller Options Trading Software
in Electronic Version with Color Charts
Order Electronic Attached Version by sending $50 Check to:
Emilie Smyth
701 E. Pine Ave. #118
Lompoc, CA

Contact Jon Schiller at
jonsch1@verizon.net
http://www.jonschilleroptions.com/
http://wwwjonschblogger.blogspot.com/

Jon Schiller Author of Options Trading Books
Self-Adaptive Options & Currency Trading
The 100% Return Options Trading Strategy
Insider's Automatic Options Trading Strategy
Compilation of Jon Schiller's OEX Options Trading Newsletters

Jon Schiller Author of Fiction Novels
Published
Masada Never Again, Multihulls
Soon to be published
Ibex, Ultra Taiwan Fighter, Lost in Space

JON SCHILLER SOFTWARE
jonsch1@verizon.net
http://www.jonschilleroptions.com/
http://wwwjonschblogger.blogspot.com/

OPTIONS PROFITS USING DECISION CHARTS

Dr. Jon Schiller

TABLE OF CONTENTS

79 Charts, 204 pages in book

Dr. Jon Schiller

Chapter 1 OEX Options Covered Credit Short Spread Strategy

I love to tell the story of how I learned the fundamentals of index option trading from a Multimillionaire: Sitting on the beach in Brest on the French Normandy coast, watching a world championship multihull regatta sail by, Bob kept his eyes glued on the team racing his 40 foot catamaran as he explained short spread option trading to me, an eager learner taking copious notes. I became even more enthusiastic when, after picking up the winning trophy, the cat's skipper told me Bob was earning about $2 million per month with his short spread strategy. That was more than two decades ago and I have since developed charts and spread sheets and have written several generations of expert system software using what I learned from Bob, plus what I've discovered investing my own capital. I have found that using Index Options for short spread trading is a safe way to earn 8% to 13% per month -- or some 96% to 156% per annum on my collateral. In addition to the option trading income, I invest the collateral used for option trading in whatever investment suits my fancy such as AAA bonds, Supranational bonds, money market funds, investment funds, or simply tech stocks. In this way the option income adds to the income from the collateral investment. You should note that only 80% of such invested capital can be counted as margin for your options trading.

The use of S&P 100 Index (OEX) covered spreads as a profitable trading strategy for me was described in my first book, The Insider's Automatic Option Trading Strategy.   I have been using this strategy for over 2 decades and have seen it work during all the market fluctuations during that time period, including some extremely spectacular rises and drops. The basic strategy: I open an equal number of **Put Covered Credit Spreads** and **Call Covered Credit Spreads** at the beginning of the new option month (first Monday after the third Friday of each month). A Put

Covered Credit Spread is selling a Put at one strike price and buying a Put the next strike price lower. I chose a **Put selling strike price** 2 standard deviations (2 sigma) below the expiration market price of the OEX. A Call Covered Credit Spread is selling a Call at one strike price and buying a Call the next strike price higher. I chose a **Call selling strike price** 2 standard deviations (2 sigma) above the expiration market price - both rounded off to the nearest 5 point strike price. The selling strike prices are called *Short Call or Short Put.* The buying strike prices are called *Long Call or Long Put.*

My software computes both the Call and Put 2 sigma values used for computing the selling strike prices for the Calls and Puts of the Covered Credit Short Spreads (CCSS).

The most significant change that has occurred in Options trading since I started 20 years ago is the advent of Internet Options Brokers such as Thinkorswim Brokers: https://www.thinkorswim.com/tos/suiteFreedom/landing-s.tos or TradeKing Brokers: http://www.tradeking.com/ . It is easy to open accounts with these website brokers. After you have opened an account and funded the account with the minimum amount for *Margin Trading* which is $2,000 you can trade Covered Credit Spreads on the broker's website. If you have software that computes the Call and Put strike prices to *sell* for the spread and the Call and Put strike prices to *buy* for the spread, it is a simple matter to *open* the two sigma Call and Put spreads using the broker's website. These websites are easy to use and below is a step by step instruction for placing an order to open Call and Put Covered Credit Short Spreads.

You can open the Put and Call Spreads simultaneously by ordering an Iron Condor which is ordered by entering the condor strike prices starting with the lowest Put increasing to the highest Call. For example, the way to place an order for 10 condors, Short C625/Long C630 & Short P535/Long P530 on TradeKing is to use their Iron Condor form as shown below for the 4 legs of the Condor in Figure 1.1:

Buy Leg 1 P530 (Lowest Strike Price), Sell Leg 2 P535, Sell Leg 3 C625 , Buy Leg 4 C630 (Highest Strike Price). The trade form has 4 regions, one for each leg of the Condor.

Action

☐ **Buy to Open** *Note: first you click on the Buy to Open - the others 3 legs are clicked automatically*

☐ Buy to Close

☐ Sell to Open

☐ Sell to Close

Contracts [ ]   *Note: You enter the Number of contracts, 10, in this box, 10 appears for the other three legs automatically*

Option0 Symbol [ ]   *Note: Enter OEB SF in leg , for the other 3 legs you must manually Enter OEB SF, OEY GE, OEY GF*

Expiration [▼]   *Note: the expiration date: 18 Jul 08 automatic appears*

Strike Price [▼]   *Note: the strike price 530 will appear, for the 1st Leg, the other leg strike prices will automatically appear when you enter the Symbols for the other 3 legs in the Symbol boxes which will be Put 535, Call 625, and Call 630*

☐ Market *Note: I rarely use market value, unless I want the Condor executed immediately*

☐ **Credit** *Note: Click on Credit, then Enter the Points for the Condor, 1.1 in the Credit box*

[ ]

Next click on the **Duration** (of the Order): Day Order.
Finally you click on **Preview Order** to obtain:
Est. Opt. Reqs: $5,000.00   Creates   Iron Condor.
Commission: $45.80

Dr. Jon Schiller

Estimated Order Total: $1,054.20

TradeKing provides the current Ask & Bid for the Condor, so you can tell the probability that the **1.1 Credit** you are asking will be filled. You can modify your asking price (**Credit**) before Punching the *Place Order* button.

See how easy to place the Broker Order, which is a once per month task, to generate a monthly profit.

Over the 2 decades I've been trading, this strategy has generated a significant monthly income, typically 10%/mo or 120%/yr on the required margin. Such a high annual return on capital permits high capital growth rates with good safety. By using spread widths of 2 sigma, one can anticipate that 9 out 10 trades will be profitable. If a sudden market fluctuation greater than 2 sigma occurs, then protective action must be taken to limit the loss from the unusual move. The Covered Credit Spread Strategy limits the maximum loss to the margin required for the spread, even if no protective action is taken. The margin required for 2 Covered Credit Short Spread = 5*100*2 = $1000. Therefore one Call CCSS + Put CCSS (the Condor) would require $1000 margin. However, I recommend that your trading capital be double the margin required, the minimum trading capital would be $2,000. So for the minimum capital in your account would allow an order of 4 contracts (options). But since I recommend you use only half of your capital for margin, you should only place an order for 2 condors. As your capital grows with your monthly profits you could increase your number of options (NOPS) which means your monthly income would rise as the NOPS increases.

Normally the protective action is to move the strike price of the threatened position, but for violent market swings, such as the raging bull market from Nov 04 through Mar 05, or the subsequent bear market from Feb 08 through Jul 08, a better strategy may be to close the threatened Put Spread at a loss, then open a debit spread. This tactic allows you to limit the loss of the threatened Put credit spread and often leads to a profit on the Put debit spread, it the market continues to drop.

My basic strategy is the *2 sigma credit double covered short spread, or Condor strategy.* In the event that the Call CCSS or the Put CCSS is threatened by the market moving too close to the Short Call or Short Put of the threatened credit spread then the threatened spread can be closed and a new spread can be opened with the *Short* at a safer distance from the Market. An alternative corrective action is to switch the short spread to a ***debit spread*** which would profit from a large move in the threatened direction.

In later chapters we will discuss the use of out-month strategies, where one uses index options beyond the current month. For example, if the current month is September, then the out-months are October, November, and December, corresponding to 2 months out, 3 months out and 4 months out, respectively. For the OEX, the strike prices are separated by 5 points, except on the out-months the separation is often 10 points. Using the out-month strategies, one can actually increase the initial credit by switching the threatened side to a wider spread and have good safety; using the current month one reduces the initial credit when widening the spread.

Over the years I have used a Personal Computer to help me make my trading decisions. A principle objective of this book is to explain the use of PC charts and spread sheets to profit from index option trading. A more complete explanation of the rationale behind my short spread trading strategy is covered in my other 3 options trading books. However, this latest book contains all the details needed to understand the strategies using Excel spread sheets and decision charts generated from these spread sheets on your PC slanted towards the PC trading environment. These spread sheets and charts are the tools you need for profitable index option trading.

- **PART 1** describes index option trading strategies and shows how to predict your capital growth in the future.
- **PART 2** gives details of how to use charts and spread sheet tools and explains the WWI triggers for both options and currency trading.
- **PART 3** describes the decision charts and spread sheets to tell

you when to use the various strategies for profitable trading.

- **PART 4** covers Internet Aids which are now available for trading and also tactics to increase your profits. This Part also discusses in detail two Excel software programs I have developed and refined over the years to aid you in options trading:

1. *SelfAdapDTN4* which includes the command center for monitoring your Covered Credit Spreads, Covered Debit Spreads, and Long Positions; a TradeForm for computing 2 sigma covered spread for OEX, AAPL, RIMM, SPY, & QQQQ; spread sheets for entering daily fluctuations; and sheets for entering CBOE options data from their free 15 minute delayed website: http://www.cboe.com/

2. *SelfAdapSigIndicOEX* which includes a spread sheet for computing the various decision and surveillance charts described in this book. A 5 input 3 level Neural Network sheet shows Trend up or down. These 2 programs are available from your author as email attachments for a modest fee.

My *SelfAdapDTN4* program uses a *Copy Special – Txt,* Excel command, for entering real time data obtained from the internet into a QteOp2 sheet. This Excel tool avoids the need to use the more complex Visual Basic that my earlier programs used or a coded actuated macro program.. A User's Manual is provided to make this program simple to use and understand. I am always available for answering questions on email: jonsch1@verizon.net .

To use these software tools developed by your author, you will need a PC with:

- Windows
- Excel
- Word
- Hard Disk with at least 8 MB free space
- Microsoft compatible Mouse

OEX Covered Credit Short Spread (CCSS) Strategy

Based on my past experience, I have found the S&P 100 Index (OEX) Options to be the best of many available index options for my credit covered short spread strategy. The OEX is best because it has both large open interest and high daily trading volume to assure liquidity.   I sell an equal number of Call and Put options at strike prices that are computed using the statistical parameter 2 sigma (2 times the OEX standard deviation).   I compute the Call 2 sigma based on the monthly maximum rise for the last 13 months; I compute the OEX 2 sigma based on the monthly   (OEX maximum – OEX minimum) for the last 13 months.   The strike price for the covered credit short spreads (CCSS) are computed from the equations below:

- Call Short Strike Price = Index Market Value + 2 Sigma, rounded to the nearest 5
- Put Short Strike Price = Index Market Value - 2 Sigma, rounded to the nearest 5

N.B. *We have to round off to the nearest 5 points because OEX strike prices are 5 points apart and I use the same 2 sigma for both Call & Put*

To open NOPS (number of options) Covered Credit Short Spreads :

- Sell NOPS 2sig Calls and Buy NOPS Calls at a strike price 5 points higher for the Call spreads
- Sell NOPS 2 sig Puts and Buy NOPS Puts at a strike price 5 points lower for the Put spreads

Normally these spreads are opened on the first Monday after the 3rd Friday expiration of the new option month, but the Call side and Put side do not have to be opened at the same time or even the same day.   If you open both Call and Put spreads simultaneously, this is called an Iron Condor.   Brokers like TradeKing have condor as one of the selections for option trade entry.   The number of options depend on the amount of capital you have in your trading account since each covered spread requires a CBOE determined margin as collateral. *I recommend never using more than 50% of your trading capital as margin.*

To illustrate this short spread strategy a numerical example is given below:

1. Assume you have a trading capital = $10,000 and the OEX has a value of 553.25.

The margin required for 1 short covered spread = 5*100 = $500 where 5 is the number of points between the short and long positions in the spread, and 100 is the dollars per point for options, or the number of 'shares' per option. The number of options, NOPS, that can be opened is given by the equation:

NOPS = Capital*50% margin/per spread = ($10,000*0.5)/($500*2) = 10

2. Assume the 2 sigma = 20, then to compute the Short Call

Short Call = Round((OEX + 2sig)/5,0)*5 = 553.25+20 = rounded (573.25) =575

Long Call = Short Call + 5 = 580, so the Call covered spread is: C575/580

Short Put = Round((OEX - 2sig)/5,0)*5 = 553.25-20 = rounded (533.25) =535

Long Put = Short Put – 5 = 530, so the Put covered spread is: P535/530.

3. Assume the Premiums for the Call and Put strike prices are given below:

C575 = 3.5, C580 =2.8, so the Call premium difference = 3.5-2.8 = 0.7

P535 = 3.2, P530 =2.6, so the Put premium difference = 3.2-2.6 = 0.6

The Condor Premium = 0.7+0.6 = 1.3

4. Assume you place the order to open both the Call Spread and the Put Spread simultaneously as a Condor, and the the Broker Commissions is $4.50 min +$0.65per option,

So the Condor commission = 10*2*2*.65+4.5 = $30.5 Compute the Covered Spread Initial Credit using the equations below

The Condor Initial Credit for 10 Condors = 10*1.3*100 – 30.5 = $1269.5

6. The Margin for the Condor = 5*10*100 = $5000;

Note: the Call spread and Put spread do not have to be opened simultaneously to receive the condor status, but the commission would be $17.5 more..

7. The %Return on Margin = Init Credit/Margin = 1356/5000 =27.12% per month, or for the Condor. *The return on Capital = 13.56% or 162.72% per Annum.*

My software SelfAdapDTN4 computes the Call & Put 2sigma OEX Spreads using the DTN.IQ Watchlist which is available using my software for the WL details and the DTN.IQ subscription, which is about $40/Mo. This example is for the 2 sigma double covered credit short spread, or Condor is taken from the SelfAdapSprds sheet of SelfAdapDTN4 opened on 21 Apr 06 for the May 06 Option Month.

See Figure 1.1 Below

SelfAdapDTN4 Trading Center

	SPX 1,251.70	Date	12-Sep-08	ATM Longs	Prm Got	Prm Now
0.9 577.71		NOPS =	2	C655	11.91	5.50
OEX Del -1.17		Comm =	$11.60	P655	11.09	4.00
OEX DTN Options			TK Cap =	$18,214	Mgn%Cap =	
577.71	-1.17	2Sig	40.02	$39,584	After OEX Trade	
CNDR NOPS = 10		NOPS =	2	OEX/SPX	SPX Del	StkPrice
2SigCall	620	2SigPut	540	0.46	2.65	43.43
OEX Crdt Spreads		Total =	$981	Condor Expir	QLD	15-Aug-08
P555/565 Wkly	1.35	0.00	$653	$1,324	$5,000	33.12%
C580/585 Wkly	1.35	-0.02	$1,328	$1,346	$1,656	$1,671
C630/635	0.35	0.05	$328	$276	33.12%	$1,656
C635/640	0.35	0.00	$328	$326	$966	$5,000
P545/540	0.66	0.60	$638	$34	$360	19.12%
C625/630	0.34	0.00	$318	$52	$5,000	
Expir 18 Sep		Total =	$956	$86	19.12%	%Ret/Mn

This trade form shows that an initial credit of $956 is received when the 10 Call625/630 and 10 Put545/540 Covered Credit Short Spreads are opened, requiring a margin of $5,000 or 50% of the trading capital. This is a monthly return on margin of 19.12% per month or 9.5% on capital yielding 114% annual return on capital. The maximum loss that could be suffered if the OEX finished above 625 or below 545 is $5,000 This maximum loss could be reduced by taking corrective action on the threatened side. If the OEX remains within the 2 sigma limits: C625 & P545, then the initial credit received or $956 would become the monthly profit. Sep 08 was a month with typical premiums so the Initial Credit, and %Returns are typical of Figure 1.2 above and could be expected during other months.

The corrective action for a threatened short Put at strike price 545 would be to close out the Put CCSS at P545/540 and open a new Put CCSS at P540/535. Typically the corrective action would be 1.0 points or a reduction of profit = 1.0*10*100+Com = $1,000+2*22 = $1,044. The rule is: Close out the threatened spread when the short Strike Price becomes In-The-Money (ITM). Similar results would occur for corrective action for a threatened short Call at strike price 625. If the short C625 were ITM, then the C625/630 would be closed and a new spread at C630/635 would be opened. **N.B.** *If a short Call or Put is ITM, at market close, then place an order to close the threatened Credit Spread during the 15 minutes between stock market closing and option trading. Avoid hoping!*

How Well Does the CCSS Strategy Work over a 3 Year Period?

The chart below shows the OEX fluctuations during a period from Nov 02 through Nov 05 or a period of 3 years. How do we know that there were extreme fluctuations in the OEX during this period? The chart shows the 200 day (yellow) and 60 day (green) moving averages relative to the OEX. As may be seen the OEX moves below the 200 daMA indicating a severe decline, and moves above the 200 daMA indicating a big rise in the market.

Figure 1.2 OEX Long Term Moving Average 60 & 200 Day

The trading results for the 2 sigma covered credit short spread (CCSS) are shown in the spread sheet below for the 3 year period Nov 02 through Nov 05. This spread sheet shows a strategy of increasing the number of options (NOPS) each time the CumPrft (cumulative profit) allows the Margin to be less than 50% of the trading capital. The example shows a beginning trading capital of $20,000 and after the 3 years of trading the trading capital has grown to $77,596, or a 3 year growth rate of 123% per annum. This numerical example showed a monthly trading loss during those months when the OEX varied outside the 2 sigma levels of the short Call or short Put of the Covered Spread.

Figure 1.3 OEX Covered Spread Profit and Capital Growth from Nov 02 thru Nov 05

OEX Covered Credit Short Spread

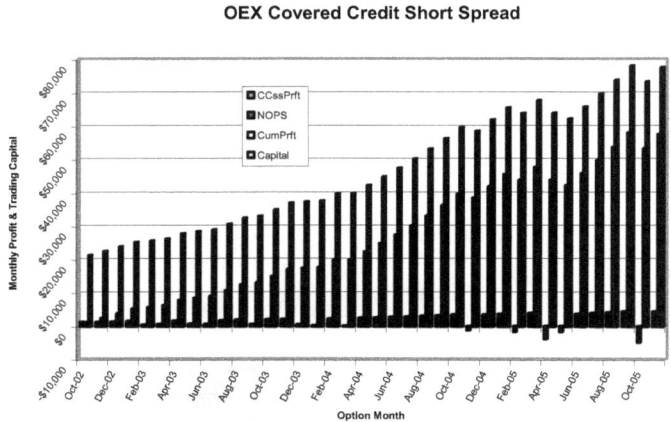

The numerical results for the first year of the three years is shown in the spread sheet below:

Figure 1.4 Spread Sheet showing Monthly CCSS Trading Results for Oct 02 thru Oct 03.

OpMo	CCssPrft	NOPS	CumPrft	$20,000 Capital
Oct-02	$1,202	10	$1,202	$21,202
Nov-02	$1,202	10	$2,404	$22,404
Dec-02	$1,322	11	$3,726	$23,726
Jan-03	$1,442	12	$5,169	$25,169
Feb-03	$404	12	$5,572	$25,572
Mar-03	$577	12	$6,149	$26,149
Apr-03	$1,563	13	$7,712	$27,712
May-03	$667	14	$8,379	$28,379
Jun-03	$505	14	$8,884	$28,884
Jul-03	$1,683	14	$10,567	$30,567
Aug-03	$1,803	15	$12,370	$32,370
Sep-03	$571	16	$12,941	$32,941
Oct-03	$1,923	16	$14,864	$34,864

As may be seen in the spread sheet above the beginning trading capital was $20,000 and after one year of trading the capital had grown to $34,864; and this was in spite of 4 months requiring corrective action in Feb, Mar, May, and Sep option months. During these four months the Market moved *above* the short Call or *below* the short Put that required corrective action.

After three years of CCSS trading the capital had grown to
:

Oct-05	-$4,779	38	$53,269	$73,269	3 yr		123%

This shows the ***average yearly growth rate = 123%*** with the trading capital growing from $20K to $73.139K. During this period the extreme fluctuations required corrective action during 12 months or 33% of the time, which was unusually high, since typically the protective actions are required about 10% of the time. When the OEX moves above the short Call or below the short Put, I recommend waiting one more trading day before taking corrective action. Often the market moves so the Call or Put is ITM then pulls back to the *safe region* less than the short Call or above the short Put. I call this the one day syndrome.

How to Protect a Threatened Call or Put Spreads

I will use the Nov 05 option month as an example of a severe monthly rise. How do I know the rise was extreme? The Call 2 sigma of the OEX for the Nov 05 = 16.65 and the Put 2 sigma = 19.72. On 21st October the OEX closed at 553.25. So the computed short Call and short Put are computed below:

sCall = 553.25+16.62 = 569.87, rounded to the nearest 5, = 570, LngCall = 570+5=575

sPut = 553.25-19.72 = 533.53, rounded to the nearest 5, = 535, LngPut = 535-5=530

In summary the OEX covered credit short spread:

sC570/575, premium difference = 0.95, for 10 Options, Initial Credit = 10*0.95*100-com = $876

sP535/530, premium difference = 0.90, for 10 Options, Initial Credit = 10*0.95*100-com = $826

Total Init = $1,702

During this option month the OEX stayed safely within the 570 and 535 bounds. On Friday 11th Nov, one week before expiration on 18th Nov, the OEX closed at 569.01, a worrisome 0.99 below the short Call at 570. Then for the next 4 days the market pulled back safely below the 570 level, until at half hour before close on Thursday 17th Nov, the day before expiration, the OEX rose to 571.13 placing the P570 into the money. This forced the prudent trader to make a corrective change by closing the sC570/575 and moving the position up by 5 points to sC575/580. The cost of closing the threatened C570/575 was 1.65 points or a cost = 1.65*10*100+74 = $1,724; the credit of opening the safe position at C575/580 was 0.25 = 10*100*.25-74 = $176. The net cost of the corrective action = 1724-176 = -$1,548.

This meant the net profit for the Nov 05 option month = $1702-$1548 = $154.

So what would have happened had we not taken corrective action?

On expiration day 18th Nov 05, the OEX closed at 574.69, meaning if the original C570/575 position had been left open, the loss at expiration would have been 574.69-570 = 4.69 points. Or a loss = 4.69*10*100+74 = $4,764 or the net loss for the trading month would have been: Expiration Loss $4764 – Initial Credit $1,702 = Nov Loss = -$3,062. Therefore, the corrective action prevented a loss and made a small profit. *So the corrective action maintained the trading capital and prevented a reduction in trading capital of over three thousand dollars.*

What Can Be Done to Protect a Threatened Put ?

A similar protective action would be taken to counter a threat to a short Put of a CCSS position. If, for example, the short Put = strike price 560 and the long Put part of the spread is at strike price 555, assume an initial credit = 0.65 when opened on the first Monday after expiration. Then the initial credit for 10 options = 10*100*0.65-22 = $622 for a Margin = 5*10*100 = $5,000. Or a return on margin = 576/5000 = 11.52% for the month or an annual return = 138%. This is typical of what may be expected for a 2 sigma Put covered spread.

Now, if during the option month that this P560/555 is open the market experiences a drop to 562, thus threatening the short

Put at strike price 560, then one would examine the decision charts for the OEX:

1. If the charts indicate this is a temporary drop and the OEX has a high probability of recovering, the threat on the short Put would be reduced. One good indicator of such a probable recovery is the Welles-Wilder Indicator being less than 20, indicating an upward movement is in the works. In this case no corrective action would be taken.

2. If the charts indicate the OEX is on a down trend, then prudent corrective action would be taken. One such indicator would be the WWI greater than 80 indicating a further drop is coming.

So What Corrective Action Would Be Taken?

The 10 short Puts at 560 would be sold to close, and the 10 long Puts at 555 would be bought to close. Such an order would be given to your broker as a Spread limit order with the close out to take place at a price of 2.4, for example. If this order were executed, the cost = 10*2.4*100+22 =$2,422, or a net loss for this position = $622 − $2422 = -$1,800. This loss could be off-set by opening a new safer Put spread at 5 points lower, or a new Put spread at short Put 555 and long Put 550. Assume you received 1.1 point for opening this new spread, so the 10 new Put covered spreads would receive initial credit = 1.1*10*100-22 = $1, 078, thus the cost $1800-$1078 = -$722 for the net cost of the corrective action in this numerical example.

Remember, *if your decision charts tell you to take corrective action, act! Don't wait and hope!*

Usually you move your threatened position by only 5 points in the safe direction. Extreme months with jumps and or drops of 3 or 4 sigma, seem to occur about once per year, and occasionally (like the 87 crash or the 91 Gulf War drop) there are enormous variations.   In Chapter 8 there is a description of how far to move your threatened Put or Call spread when threatened during extraordinary times. *You must learn to recognize these unusual happenings and take rapid action to conserve your capital* and return during the calmer periods and recoup whatever losses you may have suffered. I was trading the market during the time of the October 1987 market crash. That was a fortunate crash for Index Option Covered Credit Short Spread traders: the options expiration was on the Third Friday as usual, but the crash didn't occur until the first Monday after expiration. Since the market was acting strangely on expiration Friday, but fortunately not threatening 2 sigma CCSS positions, I took no action in the market on Monday and waited until later that trading week before venturing in the market with a new 2 sigma CCSS and received unusually high net premiums for the spreads because of the volatility.

Naked Calls & Puts Using the OEX S&P 100 Index Options

Another Strategy using Short Calls & Puts without the Covering Long Calls & Puts can be executed using Naked OEX Calls 2 sigma above the market and Naked OEX Puts 2 sigma below the market. If you execute both the short Call and short Put which I refer to as the Naked Short Spread (NSS). Most brokers require a minimum of $50,000 in your account to execute Naked Short Spreads. One popular Options Broker requires a minimum of $100,000 for Naked Short Spreads. I have learned that a London Broker, Chicago Broker, and a Swiss Broker all require a minimum account size of $50,000 to execute NSS.

I investigated the websites of some brokers which executed Naked Calls or Puts with less than the $50,000 minimum, but I believed this was an error on the trading floor and *I definitely recommend having a minimum account size of $50,000*. An example using Jan 2006 OEX options is shown below in Figure 1.5. It shows that for 10 options the total margin = $5,641 and the total Initial Credit is $1,730 giving a return on margin = 1730/5641 = 30.7%. If your broker will permit you to execute these naked short positions, this is a strategy worth considering.

http://www.interactivebrokers.com/en/accounts/smart.php?ib_entity=llc

Fig 1.5 Two Sig Naked Calls & Naked Puts using OEX

Naked Spreads	OEX =	570.00		Margin=	$5,641
shrtCallmg=	$2,501	NOPS =	10		
shrtPutmgn=	$3,140				
TotNakedMrgn=	$5,641	*Minimum Capital in Account for Naked Spreads*			
ShrtCall	Dec	Short Put		MinMrgn=	$50,000
585		555		StrkPrices	%Ret
	0.70	1.15		Prms	30.7%
$640.00		$1,090.00		Init Crdt	$1,730

What is the Algorithm for the Naked Calls and Naked Puts? The Call and Put have slightly different algorithms which are given below:

1. Naked Call Margin is given below
=1*A26+MAX((0.2*$C$20-(A25-$C$20)),0.1*$C$20,2.5*100*$D$21)

The words implemented by the Call margin algorithm are:

100% * option market value + maximum (((20% * underlying market value) - out of the money amount), 10% * underlying market value, $2.50 * multiplier * number of contracts). 20% above is 15% for broad based index options. Short sale proceeds are applied to cash.

2. Naked Put Margin is given below
=1*A27+MAX((0.2*$C$20-($C$20-C25)),0.1*$C$20,2.5*100*$D$21)

The words implemented by the Put margin algorithm are:

100% * option market value + maximum (((20% * (underlying market value) - out of the money amount), 10% * strike price, $2.50 * multiplier * number of contracts).

The margin requirements which comply with CBOE margin requirements for Naked Calls & Naked Spreads are stated below:

CBOE Margin requirement for naked Puts & Calls: Purchases of puts or calls with 9 months or less until expiration must be paid for in full. Writers of uncovered puts or calls must deposit / maintain 100% of the option proceeds* plus 15% of the aggregate contract value (current index level x $100) minus the amount by which the option is out-of-the-money, if any, subject to a minimum for calls of option proceeds* plus 10% of the aggregate contract value and a minimum for puts of option proceeds* plus

10% of the aggregate exercise price amount. (*For calculating maintenance margin, use option current market value instead of option proceeds.) Additional margin may be required pursuant to Exchange Rule 12.10.

As you may see the margin is smaller the further Out-of-The-Money the short Call of short Put is. This factor makes far OTM shorts have less margin than shorts closer to the market. Please note the hooker in the CBOE margin requirements: *Additional margin may be required pursuant to Exchange Rule 12.10.* In other words if your broker doesn't want to execute your naked Call or Put it can invoke the exception of Exchange Rule 12.10.

Why Use the OEX S&P 100 Index Options?

There are only two US Index Options that have sufficient trading volume and open interest (the total number of options open at a given time) to be considered sufficiently liquid for short spread trading. These are:

1. The OEX, code for S&P 100 index
2. The SPX, code for S&P 500 index

While I lived in Spain I traded in the London SEI options which are the American Style options based on the FTSE-100 Index. The SEI was similar to the OEX in having options with high volume and high open interest. Unfortunately, after returning to California, I can no longer trade SEI options, since traders living in the US are not permitted SEI trading. Canadian traders are permitted SEI trading, though.

High trading volume and open interest are important for successful index option trading, for the simple reason you want good liquidity when moving in and out of the options market to permit corrective changes when necessary. Also high volume and open interest reduces the danger of early assignment, which is being closed out of your CCSS position without giving an order, when either the short Call or short Put of your CCSS positions are in-the-money (ITM). Remember, ITM means your short Call is above the OEX market or your short Put is below the OEX market. Early assignment is always unpleasant, but it is particularly unpleasant if your decision charts indicate your ITM position will become safe again and you wanted to wait-it-out, without taking corrective action. Early assignment takes the decision out of your hands and places it into the market. *Early assignment would be particularly unpleasant if you held a profitable Long Call or Long Put and wanted to let the market move to make your Long Position more profitable.*

Another US Index Option for which options quotes can be obtained from the CBOE website is the XMI, which an index which tries to emulate the DJIA using only 20 stocks. This index is very unsatisfactory because is has much lower trading volume rather than the OEX or SPX. For example on Monday 21st November when XMI = 1094.02, up 2.13, the Dec P1025 only had a volume of 24 options, C1025 had zero volume, and the highest Call volume was the Jan 06 C1125 with a volume of only 10. These volumes are completely unsatisfactory for Index Options trading.

The SPX is not recommended for options because typically it has lower option volume than that for the OEX and often, one can not find strike prices 5 apart but instead 10 apart. This causes fewer options to be opened on the same amount of trading capital, therefore less initial credit would be gained.

One reason for using the OEX is that my research has shown over the past several years that OEX has smaller 2 sigma than the SPX meaning for a given amount of trading capital you may reserve higher initial credit and this higher monthly profit than for the SPX.

A word on foreign index options such as the Tokyo Nikkei 225, the Paris CAC 40 have lower open interest levels than the OEX & SPX, but more importantly, they have non American but rather European type options which *don't* allow the free changes during the option month as with US style option such as the OEX and even the London SEI. These restrictive rules do not permit free intra-month changes which are necessary to take advantage of the corrective changes described above. These rules may change in the future, but at the present time I would not recommend using

European style index options for CCSS trading, even if you are willing to take the risk that currency fluctuations involve.

If you are willing to assume Currency risks, I recommend you use the trading strategies described in my Jun 05 book, Self Adaptive Options and Currency Trading. This book describes a strategy using the Welles-Wilder Indicator (WWI) Decision Chart to determine when to buy or sell one or a fraction of Lots of Currency. Currency trading involves high leverage of your trading capital, since $1000 margin allows the buying or selling of a Lot of currency which is about $100,000. A description of Currency Trading using WWI triggers is described in Chapter 7 of this book.

What to Do During the Option Month?

Watch the stock market like a hawk! If you now have an open Short Spread Position in OEX, then your self interest is to see that the market stays less than your short Call and more than your short Put. If the OEX stays within these limits you get to keep all of your initial credit as profit. *If the OEX moves above your short Call or below your short Put, you can lose all your initial credit and part of your capital!* You always have to be ready to take corrective action for a threatened short Call or short Put during sharp rises or drops in the market. Movements greater than the 2 sigma fluctuations which take place statistically less than 10% of the time. You must watch daily for big plunges or leaps in the Index Value. In recent years the stock market has seen times of sudden market movements which require corrective action to preserve your trading capital and reduce any loss from such market fluctuations.

Rule: Close any Spread with Short Call or Short Put in IN-THE-MONEY (ITM)

Diligence is the key! In **Part 2** we will examine a number of chart and spread sheet tools to help you diligently watch the market in general and your short spread positions specifically.

Remember figure 1.2 is a chart which shows the OEX variations and it's 200 Day and 60 Day moving averages which show when the OEX moves above the 200 MAD for extreme upward moves and below the 200 MAD curve for extreme drops in the market.

The chart in Fig 1.6 below shows the difference between the 4 day and 9 day moving average relative to the OEX. On this chart are shown the Resistance levels and Support levels market in values of the OEX corresponding to these market levels and for the time period shown are: Resistance Level = 577 and Support Level = 520 or a spread of 57 points between the levels.

So the black bars of the MAD (9Da – 4Da) show that this parameter varies between plus and minus during this 3 year period. So large plus value of MAD(9-4) is indicative of a coming drop and a large negative value indicates a coming jump in the market. It may be noted that during Mar 05 when the OEX rose above the Resistance Level, this event was followed by an almost 30 point drop in a period 22 days from 7 Mar 05 to 29 Mar 05. Similarly when the OEX dropped to the support level of 520 on 12 Aug 05 this was a signal that a recovery was imminent that occurred to a rise above 545 in a little over a month. The chart also shows the 200 day moving average. Fluctuations of the OEX above this trendline shows a strong up movement. Fluctuations below this trendline indicate a severe drop. It is useful to have confirmations such as this to aid in your decision making as to what action to take in the option market.

Figure 1.6 Charts the OEX versus the MAD 9-4 market indicator

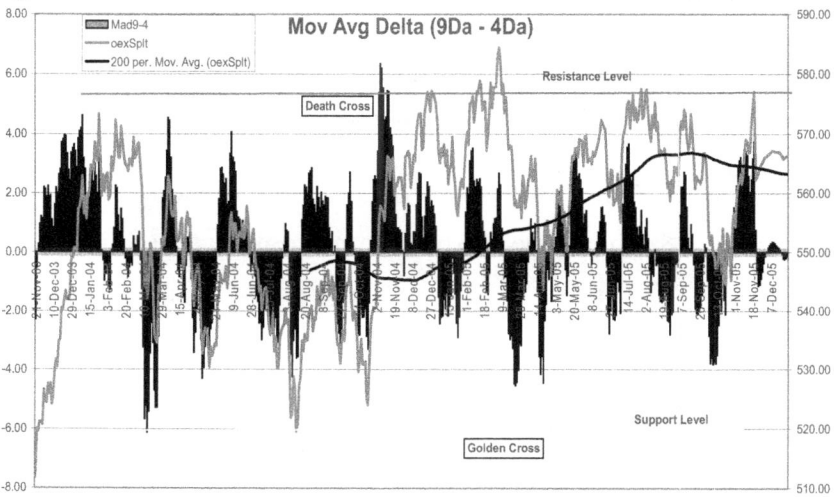

The most important spread sheets and graphical tools are listed below, as a preview to the chapters to come:

OEXmktsigIndic: This spreadsheet which is a part of the workbook SelfAdapSigIndicOEX includes daily entries of the OEX and computes signal Indicators MADC, Mad4, Mad9-4, and Sto%K-%D.

SelfAdapSprds is part of workbook SelfAdapDTN4 This spread sheet includes the OEX 2 sigma spreads for the current option month, plus other Stock 2 sigma spreads such as SPY, QQQQ, and AAPL. The OEX sheet computes the latest 13 month 2 Sig. Spread sheets are provided to allow entering the CBOE option chains for OEX and other growth stocks. The option chains can be for the current option month or future option months, for reference.

Figure 1.7 below shows a segment of this worksheet for making the daily entries and computing and displaying the 2 sigma CCSS positions. The closing date is shown as 18 Aug 08. The 2 sigma Call Spread is shown as C620/625 and the 2 sig Put Spread is shown as P540/535. For 10 Spreads the Margin is shown as $5,000 and the Initial Credit for the Condor = $525 + $588 = $1,116. The %Return on Margin = 1116/5000 = 22.32%

Figure 1.7 OEX 2 Sig Spreads for Aug 08

OEX Crdt Spreads	Total =			Condor Expir	QLD		15-Aug-08
C605/610	1.05	1.05	$1,028		-$26	$5,000	31.12%
P540/535	0.55	0.55	$528		-$26	$1,556	-$52
C620/625	0.60	0.60	$588		-$25	$1,000	58.75%

Figure 1.8a shows the 13Mo 2 sigma computation for OEX.

Mo		Max		Min	Max-Min

Jul-07	718.11	687.78	30.33
Aug-07	714.76	655.83	58.93
Sep-07	713.53	668.99	44.54
Oct-07	729.79	700.31	29.48
Nov-07	724.40	670.37	54.03
Dec-07	706.34	657.79	48.55
Jan-08	699.84	620.43	79.41
Feb-08	699.84	612.82	87.02
Mar-08	635.56	589.15	46.41
Apr-08	640.60	610.31	30.29
May-08	653.49	635.57	17.92
Jun-08	653.10	597.13	55.97
Jul-08	601.45	555.99	45.46
62.2%	**6 Mo**	**OEX 2SIG = 47.41**	
137.5%	**3 Mo**	**OEX 2SIG = 39.30**	
	13 Mo	**OEX 2SIG = 39.25**	

An important parameter used in the SelfAdapSprds work sheet is the 2 sigma or 2 standard deviations, which is computed using the Excel STDEV function. Figure 1.8a above shows the portion of the OEX spread sheet of SelfAdapDTN4 workbook which computes the 13 month 2 sigma and also the six month and 3 month 2 sigmas. As you may see for the Aug 08 option month, the 13 month 2 sigma = 39.25. This computation is updated after options expiration each month

Evaluating the OEX Spread Sheet in 2005

Instead of having daily entries the spread sheet in Figure 1.8 below, just shows the first few days of each option trading month and the last day month. The Call and Put warning signals are generated on the last day of the trading month to determine if the 2 sigma covered spread would have been safe, thus producing the initial credit as monthly profit. As may be seen from the spread sheet below, the 2 sigma CCSS finished without requiring corrective action for 3 of the 4 months. During the Oct 05 option month the OEX had a sever drop to close at expiration of 544.4. This month the short Put at strike price 550 would have required corrective action. Please note that for this Oct 05 month, if the 2 sigma CCSS had been opened on Wed 21 Sep rather than Mon 19 Sep, then the CCSS would have been for short Put 540/LngP535, then the position would have closed out worthless on expiration 21 Oct requiring no protective action. Your initial credit would have become profit for Oct 05.

Figure 1.8 Safety of 2 sigma OEX Spread Jul thru Nov 2005

15-Jul-05	575.53	0.00	0.00	595	600	555	550
18-Jul-05	571.01			590	595	550	545
19-Jul-05	574.31			595	600	555	550
20-Jul-05	576.47			595	600	555	550
19-Aug-05	566.67	0.00	0.00	595	590	545	540
22-Aug-05	567.54			590	595	550	545
23-Aug-05	565.41			595	590	545	540
24-Aug-05	580.96			590	595	540	535
16-Sep-05	573.13	0.00	0.00	595	600	555	550
19-Sep-05	570.1			590	595	550	545
20-Sep-05	566.06			595	590	545	540
21-Sep-05	560.78			590	595	540	535
21-Oct-05	544.5	0.00	1.00	565	570	525	520
24-Oct-05	553.25			575	580	535	530
25-Oct-05	552.71			575	580	535	530
26-Oct-05	550.39			570	575	530	525
18-Nov-05	558.6183	0.00	0.00	580	585	540	535

OEXSS.XLC shows 2 sigma short spread positions relative to OEX and the 20 day moving average. Figure 1.9 below as an example of results for 14 months from 16 Feb 00 thru 11 Apr 01. During this period of time corrective actions were required on the Put side as denoted on the chart. I find such charts as these very helpful in visualizing how the market is moving relative to my short Call and short Put positions of my short spreads.

Figure 1.9

STOCHASTIC %K-%D MARKET INDICATOR

Figure 1.10 below shows the complex signal indicator Stochastics %K-%D relative to the OEX with 40 day and 10 day moving average trendlines superimposed. Also shown on this decision chart are the resistance levels and support levels for the OEX. This chart is for a three year period from Nov 03 thru Nov 05. If the OEX penetrates the **Resistance line** this is the **Death Cross** meaning the market will fall back. If the OEX drops below the **Support line** this is the **Golden Cross** signaling that the market is ripe for a significant recovery.

Figure 1.10 Stochastics %K-%D Nov 03 thru Nov 06

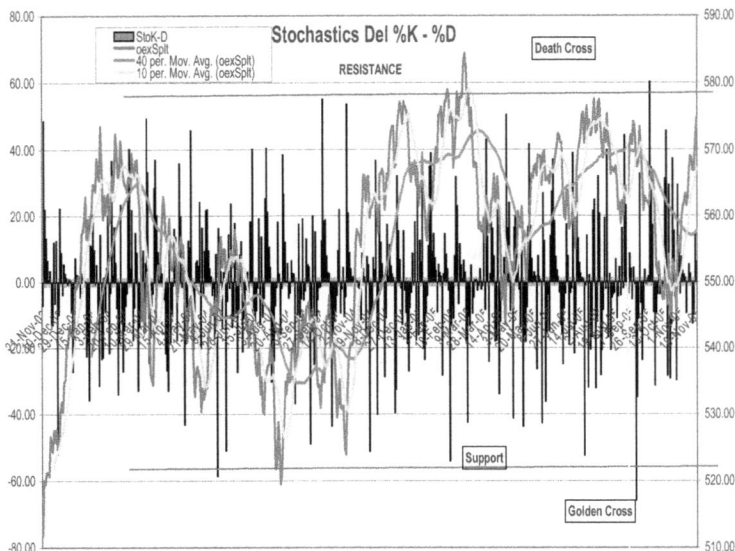

OEXURP: Unearned Profit for OEX CCSS Positions

The chart in Figure 1.11 below shows how during typical option month the unearned profit grows during the month as the premiums of the Call and Put short spreads decay. Remember, the initial credit is deposited in your trading account at the time the short spread is opened. The chart below shows how that initial credit is converted to profit during the option month. So at expiration on the third Friday, your initial credit becomes profit, provided the OEX remains below your short Call and above your short Put.

This chapter has explained the corrective actions that need to be taken should either the short Call or short Put is threatened. I still recall that when I lived in Spain and traded in London, the margin for a covered spread was only the Put side or the Call side. CBOE required both sides then, but now (2008) the US brokers only require one side instead of both sides as required previously by US brokers. The rationale for requiring only one side's margin, is that it would be impossible to lose on both sides, so only one side requires margin. This is the CBOE requirement for Condors, both sided credit spreads. This London trading rule made the %Return on margin double that than using the old US broker rules, but both London and Chicago are now the same.

Figure 1.11 Unearned Profit Growth for OEX Spreads

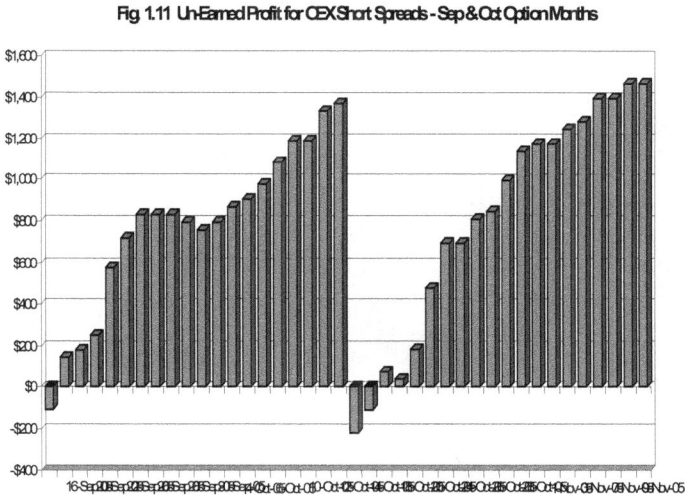

Fig. 1.11 Un-Earned Profit for OEX Short Spreads - Sep & Oct Option Months

SelfAdapDTN4 Forms for Computations for Broker Orders

Figure 1.12 in this chapter shows the Form from this Excel Workbook that computes the Covered Short Spread for the OEX including the short Call and Put and the corresponding long Calls and Puts that cover these shorts. The computations are based upon the current OEX, the two sigma computed in other spread sheets, the number of options, and the Commission.

Some of the other trade forms include:

- Change for a Threatened Call

- Change for a Threatened Put

- Narrow a covered spread by raising the Put strike price for more credit

- Narrow a covered spread by lowering the Call strike price for more credit

- Change from a short spread to a combo spread

Forms for other strategies to be discussed in later chapters of this book.

Figure 1.12 below shows a Trade Form from this work book to Open a Long Call using the Delta Strategy for a Delta = 1

Figure 1.2 Trade Form for Long Call, Delta Strategy

Open Long Call : Delta Strgy			If OEX SCH-RT indicates a Long Call				
22-Nov-05 Today's Date		Then Buy	5	Calls			
23-Nov-05 Execution Date		OEX=	579.61				
18-Nov-05 Expiration Date		NOPS=	5				
21-Oct-05 Lst Month Expir D		NDTE=	-5	L		COM/OP=	6.20
	Buy New Call SP	580					
		New Call Premium=	5.5000	Nov			
		Delta Premium=	1.0000				
			Give Order to your Broker:			At Prm or less	
	Initial Credit =	($2,788)	Buy	5 Calls at SP=	580		5.5000
			Sell	5 Calls at SP=	580		6.5000
Prft for Prm Incr =	1.00	$463					
Mo. Ret on Init Cost =	16.6%						
If Lng Call Prm drops below			4.5000 Then Sell				
If Lng Call Prm rises above			6.5000 Then Sell				

Summary

In this chapter I have shown you how to use the Decision Chart tools and Spread Sheets to do 2 sigma Covered Credit Short Spreads with a limited amount of trading capital with the goal of making that capital grow over the years.

It is how well you manage your option trading during the cataclysmic rises and falls of the market when the OEX plunges or jumps by 4 or 5 sigma in a short period of time – sometimes within a day or a few days. That will determine how rapidly your capital actually grows. I can't guarantee that you will become rich, but the spread sheet tools described in this book will help you manage the risks and become a successful, profitable short spread options trader.

Part 1 Options Trading Strategy for Capital Growth

Chapter 2 How to Make Money Investing Your Collateral?

Your broker requires collateral for your option trading when you sell options short – that is, when you open an index option short spread. You may use cash or some other investment instrument in your option trading account for the collateral. The collateral can be bonds, money market funds, stocks or any other investment with liquidity. You can make money using an investment rather than cash for the collateral. *In other words you can increase the annual income on your index options trading by overlaying the profits from the collateral investment on the options trading profits.* The down side is that typically your broker will only count 80% of your bonds or stocks, but 100% of cash for the collateral. Some brokers, such as B&J in Chicago will take 2/3 of your account funds and buy money market (MM) funds automatically without your needing to authorize each MM fund purchase. I am particularly enthusiastic about using mutual funds as the investment vehicle for the collateral. Since returning to California from Spain, I have been using some of the HiTech stocks such as Google, Yahoo, and Oracle as part of the collateral. I have used high return Mutual Funds as collateral, but some brokers permit only 50% for the value of the MF to be used as collateral for options trading (other brokers do not permit Mutual Funds in your account). TradeKing for example, has a list of Mutual Funds that they allow 100% of the value to apply to options margin.

The market correction of the spring of 1994 taught many new investors a hard lesson: bonds and mutual funds drop when the overall stock market indices drop. Veteran investors had almost forgotten the Gulf War plunge of 1990 and the 1987 crash which was comparable to the 1929 crash that set off the **great depression**. In the case of bonds in 1994, the percentage drop was greater than the percentage drop in the Dow Jones Index. The so called hedge mutual funds had an even more cataclysmic drop. I mention this fact of life – that investments are risky during stock market corrections – because during the good years of continuous bull markets, investor tend to forget there is a down side as well as an up side to market fluctuations.

Figure 2.1 shows the correlation between the 30 year mutual bond and the three stock market indices: OEX, SPX, & DJIA

Figure 2.1 Correlation between the 30 Year Bond and 3 Indi				
Correlation				
	DJIA	**30YrBnd**	**SPX**	**OEX**
DJIA	1			
30YrBnd	0.7711	1		
SPX	0.8868	0.8561	1	
OEX	0.9233	0.8233	0.9793	1

Note: the correlation between the DJIA and the long bond and the other two indices is high ranging from over 77% for the bond and almost 90% for the other two indices. The correlation between the long bond and the SPX & OEX is over 80% and the correlation between the S&P 500 and S&P 100 is 98% for the SPX and 92% for the OEX.. With these high index to bond correlations, then using Bonds for collateral is not as good a hedge as some people believe. In other words when the stock market drops the long bond drops almost the same percentage.

Trade Off of Securities Versus Cash for Options Trading Collateral

The following spread sheet illustrate five different cases for allocating your trading capital among Mutual Funds, Bonds, Money Market, and Cash to use as your options trading collateral. These five cases are displayed in Figure 2.2 below:

Figure 2.2	Percent Capital Allocation to Option Collateral			
Case	**Mutual Fnd**	**30zYrBnd**	**MnyMkt**	**Cash**
1	100%	0%	0%	0%
2	0%	100%	0%	0%
3	60%	40%	0%	0%
4	0%	0%	100%	0%
5	0%	0%	0%	100%
% ApCltrl	80%	80%	90%	100%

The five cases have different percentages of your trading capital allocated to the 4 assets. The last row in the spread sheet show the percentage that your trading capital that would be allocated to your options trading collateral. It is assumed that brokers are permitted to apply the following percentages of the assets for each type of collateral:

- 50% for Bonds & Mutual Funds
- 90% for Money Markets
- 100% for Cash

Note that for all 5 cases the % applied collateral of the mix of assets ranges from 50% for mutual funds and 30 yr bonds to 90% for money market funds up to the full 100%, of course, for cash. If you wish to use Stocks for your collateral investment (80% of their value is applicable to margin) to the possible groups of stocks are:

- Hi Tech Stocks such as Yahoo, Google, Microsoft, and Intel (during 2005 this group had a growth rate of 46%)
- Blue Chip Stocks such as IBM and GM
- Stocks in the Asian markets of Tokyo, Singapore, and Hong Kong
- Other more speculative stocks such as on the South American markets or small Capitalization stocks

Mutual Fund Investment Strategy – Overview

I believe the best strategy is to select a family of funds such *Fidelity* which has a wide variety of funds for every conceivable objective and select from this family the few funds you want to consider. I assume that most people trading options (the readers of this book, for example) would select an aggressive growth fund to invest their option trading capital and buy and hold thus permitting the Fund Manager to take the necessary action when there is a downward movement in the market.. This allows you to concentrate on Options trading and let the fund manager to adjust the fund when there is a market downward correction. Based on the charts later in this chapter the fund managers do a good job of correcting the funds for market fluctuations.

The table in Figure 2.3 below compares the five US mutual fund families listed below.

Mutual funds occur in family of funds such as:

- Fidelity, with 115 funds, which is one of the largest families in the US
- Dreyfus, with 18 funds
- Benham, with 22 funds
- Scudder, with 24 funds
- Vanguard, with 53 funds

The largest fund manager in the world is Union Bank of Switzerland, which is headquartered in Zürich. I am fond of UBS because they were my first options broker when I started trading options while I lived in Spain. According to the Wall Street Journal, UBS has 84 funds in a variety of currencies including US$, Swiss Franc, Deutch Mark, Yen, and more recently the Euro. US traders can not purchase these UBS funds, but perhaps some of my European readers may be interested in these bonds as an investment for their trading capital as well as a hedge against currency fluctuations. They will also learn there are no taxes on trading profits for Non-Swiss citizens.

The table in Figure 2.3 below compares the five US Mutual Fund Families listed using the time period from 19 Feb 1993 through 3 May 94 because it included the severe downward correction which I call *the Spring 94 correction.* The column to the right lists the best fund for the family. As you may see Fidelity and Benham best funds (FLATX & BGEIX) both have annual returns over 33%. You may not want to select the best fund for the family because it would be too volatile and cause you to switch out of the fund too often. However it would be nice to have a fund that had an annual return one third the annual return of OEX Covered Credit Spread trading. For example BGEIX is a gold earning fund and gold is very volatile. My research indicates that it should be possible to buy a fund with an annual yield of 20% without any problem.

I should point out that if you stick with funds within the same family, you should be allowed to switch funds a few times per year without paying any commission. I favor using the Fidelity family and their best funds are Magellan Fund, FLATX, which uses Latin funds from Argentina.

Figure 2.3 Comparison of MF Fanilies

Family	#Fnd	Avg Fnd	Best Fnd	BF Symb
Fidelity	115	11.8%	33.4%	FLATX
Benham	22	4.3%	33.6%	BGEIX
Scudder	24	10.0%	25.7%	SCINX
Vanguard	53	7.7%	24.4%	VEURX
Dreyfus	18	6.6%	19.7%	DSAIX
	Avg =	8.1%	27.4%	

COMPARISON OF FLATX With SPX

Figure 2.4 below compares the FLATX fund with the SPX index. As may be seen the fund growth rate is much higher for FLATX than for SPX during the 2005 year with the FLATX growth greater than 60% for the first 11 months of 2005 compared with the S&P 500 growth rate of about 8% year to date for 2005.

Dr. Jon Schiller

Yahoo financial page is a convenient way to get the comparison of the mutual fund with the SPX (Yahoo refers to SPX as ^GSPC).

COMPARISON OF FLATX With SPX

Figure 2.4 below compares the FLATX fund with the SPX index. As may be seen the fund growth rate is much higher for FLATX than for SPX during the 2005 year with the FLATX growth greater than 60% for the first 11 months of 2005 compared with the S&P 500 growth rate of about 8% year to date for 2005.

Yahoo financial page is a convenient way to get the comparison of the mutual fund with the SPX (Yahoo refers to SPX as ^GSPC).

FIG 2.4 Comparison of FLATX with SPX (GSPC)

Figure 2.7 FLATX market variations compared with the SPX over the first 5 years of the 20th Century

Please Note: If you use FLATX for your collateral with TradeKing brokers, only 70% of the value can be used as your

Margin for Spreads. Note: I tried once in 2008 to buy FLATX with TradeKing and they refused to permit buying.

COMPARISON OF BGEIX With SPX

Figure 2.5 below also obtained from the Yahoo financial services compares Benham's best fund (BGEIX) with SPX. As you may see BGEIX had a big drop early in 2005 and rose at the end of Nov 05 be almost equal to SPX in year to date growth.

Fig 2.5 Comparison of BGEIX with SPX (GSPC):

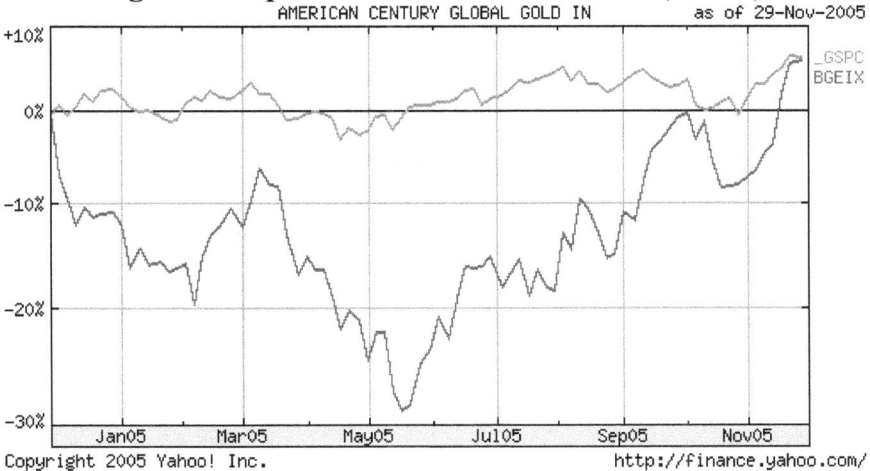

COMPARISON OF SCINX With SPX

Figure 2.6 compares SCINX with SPX, a chart taken from Yahoo financial chart service. As you may see SCINX has grown 15% per annum compared with 6% growth year to date for SPX (^GPSC in comparison chart). As you may see, SCINX correlates well with the SPX. When the SPX has drop, the SCINX has a similar drop. When SPX has a recovery or rise, the SCINX has a similar recovery:

Fig 2.6 Comparison of SCINX with SPX (GSPC)

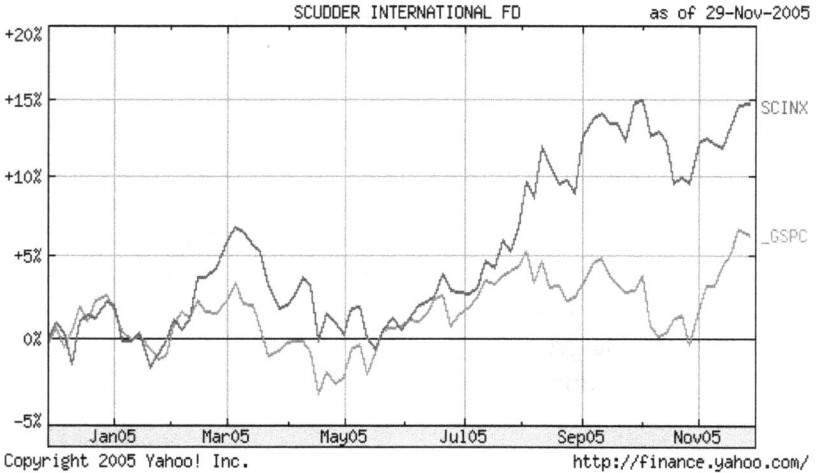

As may be seen by the charts in Figure 2.4, Fig 2.5, and Fig 2.6, FLATX is the best of the trio including BGEIX, SCINX during 2005 with the following summarized:

- FLATX   68% growth for 11 months 63.04 −1 Jul 08
- SCINX   15% growth for 11 months 63.30 − 1 Jul 08
- BGEIX   8% growth for 11 months 23.35 − 1 Jul 08

As may be seen the average annual growth rate averages 30.3% for the above trio of mutual funds compared with 30.9% in the decade old table of Fig 2.3. So the long term growth rate was consistent for the surviving trio of funds.

The other two Funds VEURX & DSAIX listed in the table of Figure 2.3, are no longer listed on the Yahoo financial services quote. So it appears that the best 3 of the 5 survived the decade from May 94 thru Nov 2005, but the 2 with lowest return of the quintet did not survive. I was pleased to find out that the surviving trio Funds listed above are quoted on the DTN.IQ realtime quote service as well as being charted and quoted by the Yahoo financial services website:

http://finance.yahoo.com/q/bc?s=FLATX&t=1y&l=on&z=m&q=l&c=

and the MarketWatch website:
http://www.marketwatch.com/portfolio/view.asp?siteID=mktw&UID

I recommend you remain invested in any fund you may chose to place in your option trading account funds, rather than using the trading signals to move in and out with the fluctuations of the fund. I recommend the FLATX fund, since it has been the winner of the top 3 funds for the last decade. *You should note that only 70% of the value of the FLATX Mutual Fund is applicable to Options Trading Margin, TradeKing has other Mutual Funds for which they allow 100% for Margin and TradeKing did not permit me to invest in FLATX..*

The market indicators will be discussed in more detail in Chapter 7. I have an Excel workbook: SelfAdapSigIndicOEX which has the decision indicators computed and charted for OEX. This work book also includes a spread sheet for entering the daily closing prices for the OEX and also has a Neural Network for indicating the market trend: Up or Down. This Neural Network indicator is presented in Fig 8.1 in Chapter 8 below. When the Neural Network >10 OEX is in an Uptrend. When the Neural Network <10 OEX is in a Down trend This workbook is given gratis to any of my readers who purchase my latest OEX workbook: SelfAdapDTN4 which may be ordered for $70 by emailing me at jonsch1@verizon.net, the files will be sent as email attachments to the email of my readers who may so order.

YAHOO MUTUAL FUND DATA

There has been a wealth of information with all of the details of mutual funds on the Internet which wasn't available when I first started researching funds while I lived in Spain during the early 1990s. For example a website which contains information about *all* mutual funds are given in the following website: http://biz.yahoo.com/edu/ed_fund.html
This website includes the following types of information:

- Mutual Fund Tools including *the top performers*
- Mutual Fund Resources including *funds by family* with hundreds listed alphabetically. Each Fund has data such as the historical charts and details of the fund
- Mutual Fund Websites, including *references and guides*

This website also acts as a learning center for mutual funds including the following:

- Overview including *mutual fund basics*
- Interactive tools including Asset Allocation Planner
- Types of mutual funds
- Fund Strategies
- Tax Efficiencies

This website has so much information that it could comprise a complete book. I will just show you data I obtain about FLATX, the best performing of the mutual funds described in this chapter.

in summary the Yahoo website for Mutual Funds presents a huge amount of data on a very large number of mutual funds. The good news is the data is updated daily!

The TradeKing approved Newsletter for use with their AutoTrade service is Disciplined QQQ Trading in Jul 08 has introduced an ETF (Exchange Trade Fund) newsletter:

Disciplined ETF Trading Newsletter which for short term Fund investing. The ETF funds they picked on 20 Jul 08 are summarized below: in **Figure 2.7 Review of NL Picks**

ETF	Type	Position	Mkt Rel Mon Open	Fri Cls	%Prft
XBI	BioTech Lng	Long	61.51	62.99	2.4%
SKF	UltraSFin Lng	Shrt	166.5	138.0	-17.1%
PEY	HiDivAch Shrt	Short	8.34	9.09	- 8.6%

Holding the Fund position for a week would have lost on 2 of the 3 funds.

Part 1 Options Trading Strategy for Capital Growth

Chapter 3 Chaos Patterns for Long Strategy Wins

The OEX market fluctuations appear to be chaotic, that is pattern without logic. Our basic short credit spread strategy is to overcome this chaos by using the 2 sigma measurement to estimate how much the OEX will rise and fall during the options month and select our short Call and Put strike prices to be outside the estimated fluctuation. Chaos theory tells us that within seemingly chaotic motions of the market there may be patterns that we can use to develop strategies for trading. There is a great deal of research underway using sophisticated software programs to detect such patterns. This software follows under the general heading of *Artificial Intelligence* with a number of sub-areas including:

- Neural Networks
- Genetic Algorithms
- Chaos Theory
- Fuzzy Logic
- Knowledge Based Systems

The software I have developed is best classified as a *Knowledge Based Trading System* based on knowledge accumulated during 2 decades of index options trading. I've detected trading patterns (using human neurons) which can be used to augment the profits from short spread trading. These patterns lead to low risk, high potential profit strategies. The strategies involve taking a long position using ATM (At-The-Money) Calls or Puts, and then after one or two days, closing out the position with a good profit return.

Long Put First 2 Day Strategy for Bear Leg- Switch to Long Call in Bull Leg

When the market switches from a Bear Leg to a Bull Leg,, then the strategy switching from the *long Put changes to long Call first 2 day strategy* has the potential of increasing your monthly income by switching from Long Puts to Long Calls. For the 2 year time period from Jun 06 through Jun 08 the strategy of buying ATM Puts at the end of the expiration Friday for the next option month and selling the Calls at the end of the second trading day of the new option month made money for this strategy. *The problem is recognizing when the Market switches from a Bear to a Bull Leg.*

The *long Put first 2 day strategy* has the potential of increasing your monthly income by using a small fraction of your capital to buy Puts, when the Market is in a Bear leg. For the three year time period from Nov 02 through Nov 05 the strategy of buying ATM Puts at the end of the expiration Friday for the next option month and selling the Puts at the end of the second day of the new option month made money for this strategy. The results of the 3 year period showing the drop of the OEX for the first 2 days of the option month are shown in *Figure 3.1* for a time Period of for 37 months is shown below:

Figure 3.1

	Drop First two day of OpMo	
	Up	**Down**
Avg =	4.81	-7.68
No Times	16	23
%Time	41.0%	59.0%

As may be seen from the figure above, the tendency to drop the first two days of the option month is strong, dropping 59% of the time while rising 41% of the time, meaning we are in a Bear Leg of the market. The average drop was 7.68. while the average rise was 4.81 points. If we use a model to estimate the profit and loss of the Long Puts, the Long Put first 2 day strategy predicts a profitable outcome.

The profit results for the percentage time Up and Down for the above figure are evaluated using a model describe below, but provide a Profit = $,1789 requiring an Investment =$3,881, thus resulting in a return on Investment = 46.1%.

The model used for this estimated profit is given by the equation below:

=-C45*C46*100*0.5, where C45 and C46 contain the average change in OEX and the number of times the OEX dropped during the 3 year period. The factor 0.5 is the assumed slope of Put premium per point change in OEX and the 100 factor is the dollars per point for options. Please note you lose during 41% of the time the OEX rises during the first two days. The average drop is greater than the average rise, therefore the Net Profit is positive using the model.

An example of the first two day Put strategy for the Oct 05 option month with 5 Put options opened just after expiration on 16 Sep 05 is given for the Average drop, and to the left is for the 5 Call options from Jun 06 expiration to after close on Mar 08, 2 days of the OpMo on Mar 08   below:

- Bear Avg 2 day drop = 7.68   Bull   Avg   2 day rise = 4.43
- The OEX = 573.13, the ATM Put was strike price = 575
- The P575 Put premium =   7.7, cost of 5 P575 = 5*100*7.7+31 = $3,881, incl $31 com.
- At Close on Tue 19 Sep 05, the OEX = 566.06, Put 575 = 11.4, value of 5 P575 = 5*100*11.4-31 = $5,670
- *Profit of the First 2 Day Put Strategy = 5970-3881 = $1,789*
- *%Return on Investment of $3881 = 46.1%*

As you may see from the above example when this strategy works the return on investment which lasted only two trading day, is high.

Long Put Third Monday 1 Day Strategy

The Long Put third Monday 1 Day strategy can also increase your monthly trading profits by using a small fraction of your trading capital to buy Calls. For the three year time period from Nov 02 through Nov 05 the strategy of buying 5 ATM Calls at the end of the Friday before the third Monday after the Friday expiration, then sell the 5 Calls at market close the third Monday (1 trading day later). The Call strike price should be nearest strike price just above the market close the previous Friday. This strategy is profitable about 70.3% of the time.

The results of the 3 year period showing the rise of the OEX for the third Monday of the option month are shown in *Figure 3.2a & Figure 3.2b* below:

Figure 3.2a

	Down	Up
No Times	23	16
No Options	5	
Profit =	$8,836	-$3,851
Net Prft =	$4,985	

Figure 3.2b

	Down	Up
No Times	13	9
No Options	5	
Profit =	$8,836	-$7,221
Net Prft =	$1,615	

As may be seen from the table in Fig 3.2a the 3rd Friday has an up movement of the OEX 70.3% and a down movement 26.7%. If we use the same model (as used for the first 2 day drop) to estimate the profit and loss of the Long Calls, using the 3rd Monday Chaos pattern rise, the model predicts a profitable outcome as shown by the Figure **3.2b** below:

- *Profit = $1,615*
- *%Return on Investment of $2281 = 70.8%*

As you may see from the above example when this strategy works the return on investment which lasted only one trading day, is high.

Long Call Last 2 Days Strategy

The long Call last 2 day strategy is a third way to increase your monthly trading profits by using a small fraction of your trading capital to take a long Call position for a short time. For the three year time period from Nov 02 through Nov 05 the strategy of buying 5 ATM Calls for the Next Option Month at the end of the Wednesday before the third Friday expiration, then sell the 5 Calls at market close after expiration (2 trading day later). The Call strike price should be nearest strike price just above the market close on that Wednesday.

The results of the 3 year period showing the rise of the OEX for the last 2 days of the option month are shown in *Figure 3.3a* below:

Figure 3.3a

Figure 3.3a

Figure 3.1a

	Drop	First two day of OpMo
	Up	**Down**
Avg =	4.81	-7.68
No Times	16	23
%Time	41.0%	59.0%

As may be seen for this 3 year period, the last 2 day rise of this Chaos pattern occurred 59.0% of the time, not as good as the 70% for the first 2 day drop and 3rd Monday rise of the other two Chaos patterns. Another bad factor is the average down was 6 and the average up was 3.9. As a result the profit using the same model as the other two Chaos patterns was not as good, as shown below in *Figure 3.3b* below:

Figure 3.3b Last 2 Da Nx OpMo

	Down	**Up**
No Times	26	11
No Options	5	
Proft =	$4,338	-$4,571
Net Prft =	-$232	

The model showed that this pattern had a small loss during the 3 year period. Profit results for the above 2 day strategy can be significantly improved by making sure that the WWI is less than 20 before executing this long position.

An example of the last two day Call strategy for the Nov 05 option month with 5 Put options opened just after close on Wednesday 16 Nov 05 is given below:

- The 2 day rise = 7.76
- The OEX = 566.93, the ATM Call was strike price = 565
- The C565 premium = 3.7, cost of 5 C565 = 5*100*3.7+31 = $1,881, incl $31 com.
- At Close on Fri 18 Nov 05, the OEX = 574.69, Call 565 = 9.7, value of 5 P575 = 5*100*9.7-31 = $4,819
- ***Profit of the Last 2 Day Strategy = 4819-1881 = $2,938***
- ***%Return on Investment of $1881 = 156.2%***

As may be seen from the above example, when the last two day Call strategy works, the results can be very satisfactory. In two trading days, the profit was 50 percent more than the investment.

Buy-Sell Indicators Improve Chaos Pattern Profits

There are two widely used buy-sell indicators that can be used to decide when to execute the long strategies described above. The first is the Moving Average Difference, MAD indicator , and the second more complex indicator it he so called Moving Average Convergence Divergence, MADC. However, over the years I've grown to favor the 7 Day Welles-Wilder Indicator (WWI), for the simple reason that it gives a strong indication if the OEX is likely to Drop or Rise. The Drop signal is WWI > 80; The Rise signal is WWI < 20.

1. So for example for the Last Two Days of the OpMo Call Strategy would be a trigger to execute if at the close of Wednesday before the 3rd Friday expiration

if the WWI < 20. This would mean the Chaos pattern is re-enforced by the WWI signaling that a rise is predicted.

2. For the First 2 days of the OpMo Put Strategy would be encouraged if at close on expiration Friday the WWI > 80, which indicates the OEX is ready for a drop. Again the WWI re-enforces the Chaos pattern of a drop the first two days of the option month.

3. The 3rd Monday Call strategy would be more likely to be profitable if the WWI < 20 at close on the Friday before the third Monday, thus confirming the Chaos pattern..

The 7 Day WWI for the OEX is plotted on the same chart as the OEX and the 20 day and 200 day moving averages. See Figure 3.3c below for this chart for the time period Nov 04 through Dec 05.

Fig 3.3c OEX vs WWI, 20 Day MA, 200 Day MA & Linear Trendlines

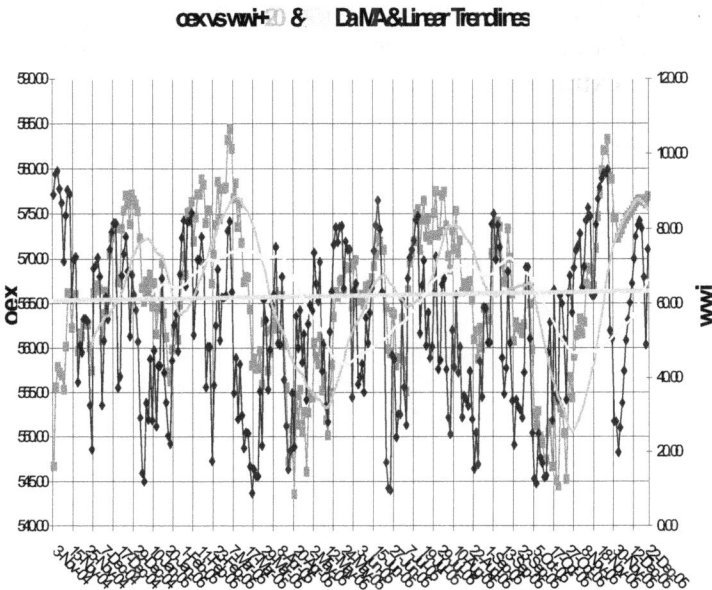

oex vs wwi+ & DaMA&Linear Trendlines

In the above chart the purple curve is the OEX and the black curve is the WWI. The blue trendline is the 20 Day moving average and yellow line is the 200 Day moving average. The Green trendline shows that for the year covered by this decision chart that the OEX had almost no trend up or down. Note that when the OEX rose above the 200 Day MA, this was a strong signal for an impending downward correction. Likewise a strong drop below the 200 D MA is another strong signal for a coming recovery. Such a drop occurred in Mar 05 and a recovery occurred in Oct 05.

In summary you may improve your Covered Spread monthly profits by using the Chaos patterns confirmed by the WWI. In other words if a short term Chaos Put pattern is re-enforced by a WWI > 80, then the pattern trade is more probable to profitable. If a short Chaos Call pattern is re-enforced by a WWI < 20, this pattern trade is more likely to show a profit.

Summary of Chaos Pattern Trades over 3 Year Period

The three Chaos pattern trade strategies discussed in this chapter are shown for the 3 years from Nov 02 through Nov 05 are shown in Figure 3.4 below. It should be noted that the Figures 3.1, 3.2, and 3.3 were extracted from this overall chart.

Figure 3.4   Profit Analysis of Chaos Using 5 Options

OpMo	First two day of OpMo		Third Mon of OpMo		Last 2 Days of OpMO	
	Up	Down	Up	Down	Up	Down
Nov-02	3.57		4.10		13.11	
Dec-02		-6.03		-1.66	2.68	
Jan-03		-2.19	10.54			-9.52
Feb-03		-7.01	3.13		1.07	
Mar-03		-4.99		-10.48	11.52	
Apr-03		-11.59	0.56		6.96	
May-03	9.32			-2.58	1.74	
Jun-03		-12.14	2.16			-7.26
Jul-03		-5.90	9.42		0.43	
Aug-03		-3.86	1.86		3.01	
Sep-03	5.62		7.50		5.19	
Oct-03		-4.50	1.87			-4.02
Nov-03	3.64		4.03			-5.05
Dec-03	7.77		1.80		5.06	
Jan-04	3.16		7.32		4.95	
Feb-04		-0.97	2.45			-3.46
Mar-04		-1.18		-4.78		-7.80
Apr-04		-8.53	4.76		0.23	
May-04	3.31		4.97		2.05	
Jun-04	8.06		8.61		1.38	
Jul-04		-1.34		-1.84		-5.89
Aug-04	3.75		2.74		1.20	
Sep-04		-1.06		-3.09	3.17	
Oct-04		-1.06	1.63			-3.68
Nov-04		-0.81		-0.15		-6.03
Dec-04	1.60			-0.49		-6.08
Jan-05	5.99			-2.96		-6.57
Feb-05	2.55		0.18			-2.82
Mar-05		-8.17	1.20		0.53	
Apr-05		-9.87	2.00			-13.06
May-05	3.72		2.03		2.24	
Jun-05	1.93		0.26		3.19	
Jul-05		-1.31	4.46		3.57	
Aug-05		-1.22	0.41			-0.61
Sep-05		-1.26		-1.21	5.72	
Oct-05		-7.07		-1.84		-9.56
Nov-05	8.21		1.33		7.76	
Dec-05		-13.19				
Jan-06						
2sig=		8.11	6.00		5.64	
Avg=	4.81	-7.68	3.51	-2.83	3.94	-6.09
No Times	16	23	26	11	22	15
%Time	41.03%	58.97%	70.27%	29.73%	59.46%	40.54%
Estim Pft	-$3,851	$8,836	$4,566	-$1,554	$4,338	-$4,571
NOPS	Net Pft =	$4,995	$3,012		$232	

Part 1 Options Trading Strategy for Capital Growth

Chapter 4 How to Profit from Big Market Changes

The short credit spread strategy yields consistent profits when the market fluctuations during the option month are less than the 2 sigma which occurs 90% of the time. Fortunately, large jumps and plunges in the market do not occur very frequently, typically once per year or less. To provide you an overview of such large rises and falls over a 5 year period, the chart in Figure 4.1a below shows the 5 year period from Oct 01 through Oct 05:

The chart of Fig 4.1a above shows there was one major market collapse in the Spring of 2002, a major recovery one year later, a descent during Spring of 2004 and a significant recovery during Winter of 2004. During the Spring of 2005 there was a 6% drop and a 5% recovery during the Fall of 2005. So during this 5 year period there was one major collapse and recovery and 4 significant descents and recoveries. It is difficult to remain in Short Credit Spread positions when there are large, rapid changes; we need a strategy to switch from Short Credit Spreads to a strategy that makes high profits with these rapid drops and rises. I will discuss two such strategies:

- Combo Spread Strategy
- Debit Spread Strategy

A Chart showing the OEX for the period May 07 thru Aug 08 is shown below in Figure 4.1b:

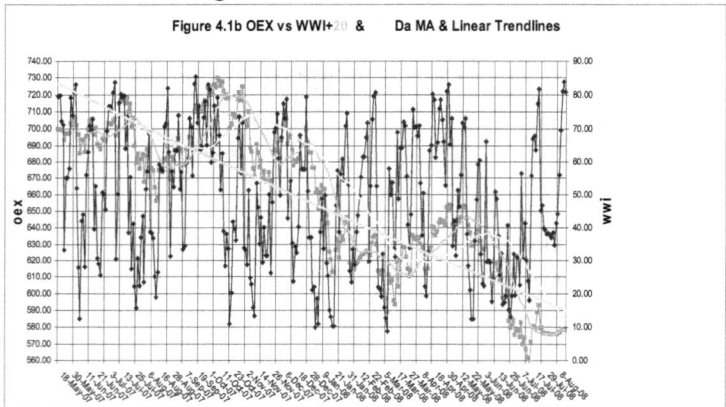

Figure 4.1b OEX vs WWI+20 & Da MA & Linear Trendlines

The down trend line shows a strong down trend during this period, with a strong drop during the Feb 08 option month. The 200 day exponential moving average shows that the OEX dropped far below the 200 MA, meaning the market was oversold and ready for a recovery which occurred during the August 08 option month.

I find referring to these charts in my SelfAdapDTN4 software package to maintain my orientation as to what the market is doing. Remember you may obtain an E-version of this book in full color by sending an email to me and a check for $50 to Emilie Smyth.

Combo Spread Strategy: Long Call/Short Put or Long Put/Short Call

Switching to the right type of combo spread can help us profit from the big moves. One strategy I have found that works well is to switch from a short spread to a combo spread when the market sentiment changes because of one of these big, rapid moves. A combo spread of a long Put and short Call is used for drops; a combo spread of a long Call and short Put is used for jumps.

In such big market moves, if we keep a short spread and make defensive moves, we will end up losing. For example, during the Spring 1994 correction, the OEX dropped 29.41 points during the April 94 option month, or some 7.6 sigma. A two sigma short spread opened for April 94 and with the Put covered spread held and changed defensively would have lost heavily. But by switching the Put covered spread to a Combo Spread: long Put and short Call, a handsome profit was made. Profit, not loss – that's the name of the OEX option trading game.

The big question is how do we know when to switch from the dual short spread (or Condor) to the Combo Spread with a long Put or Call. The answer is: we use market indicators to help make the decision that the market has really changed and we should switch when so signaled. Above in Figure 4.1b I showed how the 200 Day MA can show when the market is badly oversold, thus ripe for a recovery. In chapter 3 I mentioned three market indicators – the MAD (moving average difference) and the MADC (moving average difference convergence) and the WWI (Welles-Wilder Indicator), a relative strength indicator)– to help tell when to make the 1 or 2 day Long Call or Put trading strategies. Those strategies were used in parallel with the short credit spreads to augment the monthly trading income. The Combo strategy is used to switch from the short spread to a combo spread to profit big from a big change in the OEX during the whole option month. We used the MAD, MADC, and WWI to predict the market change during that Spring 1994 correction. Using these indicators you would have been able to decide when to switch from a short Put covered credit spread to a Combo Spread: long Put and short Call.

Dr. Jon Schiller

You must read the indicator and decide decisively and quickly. Waiting one or two days can be very costly when there is a big drop. Drops happen faster than rises – drops in *days*, rises in *weeks often happens*.

Figure 4.2 OEX & 4 Day MAD below:

Mad4 & OEX

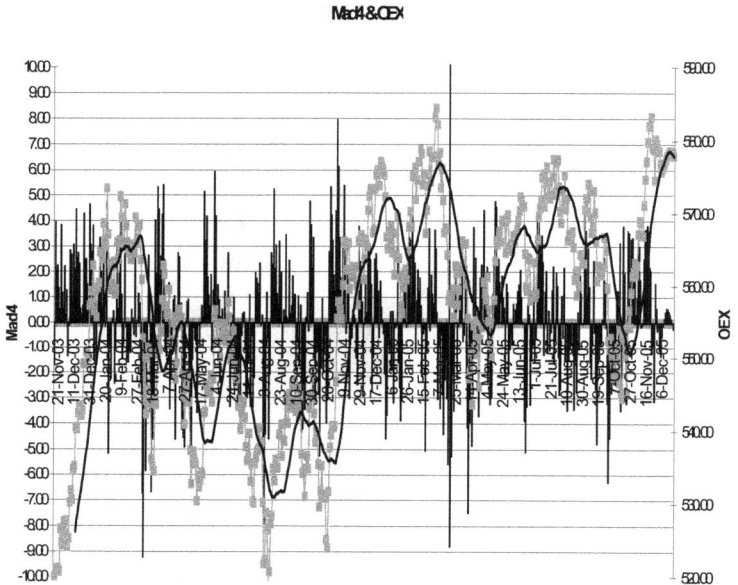

Please note that, during the March 05 correction, the MAD4 rapidly showed the drop from 584.43 to 567.94 (-16.46 points) from 7 Mar 05 to 18 Mar 05 (Mar Expir.), in 10 trading days - an average drop of 1.65 points per day. The MADC dropped from 0.79 and reached -.37 on 16 Mar. The WWI was 81.97 on 7 Mar indicating the OEX was overbought and ripe for a drop. The signal was that at this time the Short Put at 565 *might* be threatened before expiration on 18th Mar 05. At expiration, the OEX = 567.94, therefore if the Short Put spread and Short Call spread at been held until expiration both would have expired worthless, which would have meant the shortC590/LongC595 with initial credit = 0.5 points and the shortP560/LngP555 with initial credit of 1.15 would have been the profit for the option month.

But, as the Figure 4.3 below shows, the actual value for closing the Short Put and opening a new Combo spread LP585/sC580 which cost 2.7 points, at expiration yielded a profit of 17.06 points. At the level of 10 options for the month, the net profit at expiration = $14,286 compared with only $1,002 from the Condor: Call and Put short credit spreads held to expiration.

Please see the switch from Put Covered Credit Spread to the Combo LP585/sC580 when the WWI and MAD4 signaled a drop was coming on 7th Mar 05, displayed in Fig 4.3 below:

Figure 4.3	NOPS	10									
	2sig=	15									
Date	OEX	CallCCSS	sCPrm	Call InitCrdt	PutCCSS	sPPrm	Put InitCrdt	Total IC	Combo	PrmCmbo	Cost Cmbo
18Feb05	575.42	C590/595	0.5	$4.26	P580/555	0.65	$5.76	$1,002	Lput sCall		
7Mar05	584.43								LP585sC580	-2.7	-$2,774
18Mar05	557.94									17.06	$16,986
Pfit Mar Option Mtr		$14,286									
Pfit if CCSS Held		$1,002									

The table in Figure 4.3 shows all the details of the change which was signaled by the WWI = 81.97, the MAD4 =2.9 and the MADC = 0.79. I felt the main signal for this switch from the short Put spread to the short Put/ Long Call Combo was the strong signal from the WWI that the OEX was badly overbought (WWI>80) meaning that a severe drop was imminent.

The WWI Figure 4.4 and MADC Figure 4.5a are shown below:

Fig 4.4 below also shows the 20 Day Moving average and the 200 Day MA and on the 7th Mar 05, the OEX was below these two indicators.

Dr. Jon Schiller

oex vs wwi+   &   DaMA&LinearTrendlines

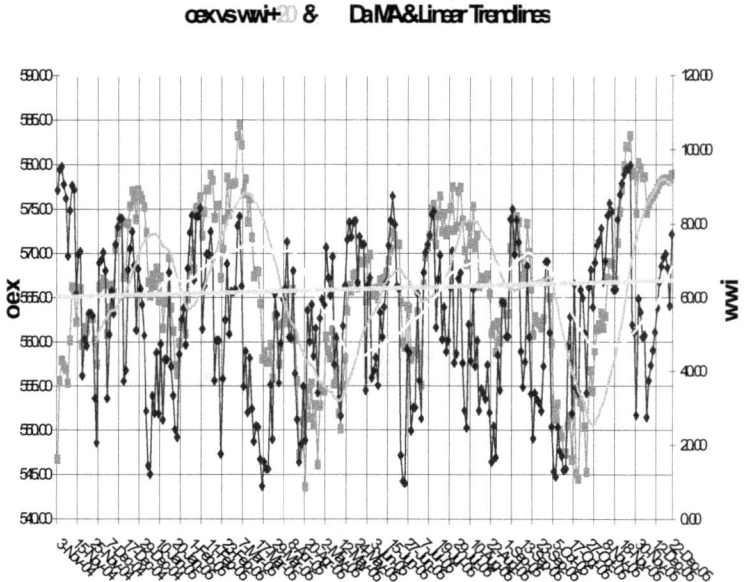

As may be seen by the OEX & MADC plot (the black bars) on Figure 4.5 below, the MADC was negative during most of the March 05 downward correction. The MADC moved positive during the May 05 recovery from the April fall. Also the Sep-Oct 05 downward correction is also shown negative by MADC. Note: SelfAdapDTN4 and SelfAdapSigIndicOEX excel workbooks, which contain the above charts, are available from your author's website: http://www.jonschilleroptions.com/

Fig 4.5 MADC & OEX Chart below:

MADC&OEX

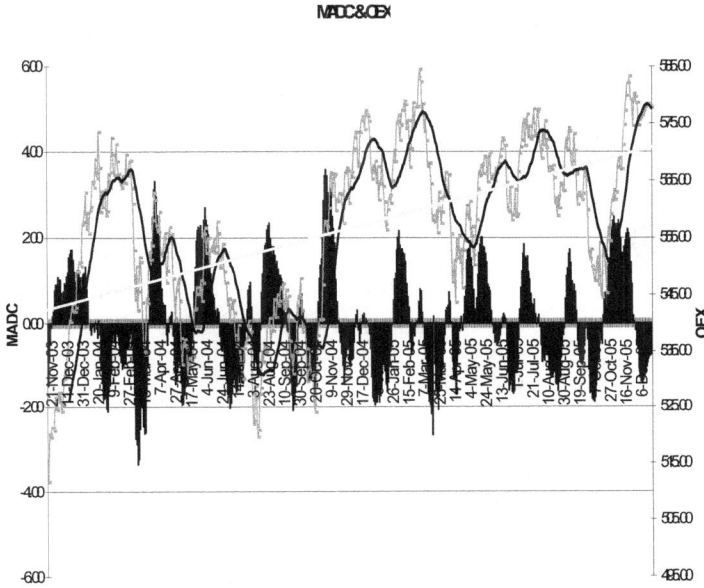

ATM Long Strategy: Long Call or Long Put Triggered by WWI

The ATM (At-the-Money) Long strategy is an alternate strategy to the Combo Spread to be used to profit from big jumps with a Call ATM Long. The long Call closest to the market is used when the WWI < 20 meaning the market is oversold ready to rise.

A Put Debit Spread generates a profit from large drops. The long Put closest to the market is used when the WWI > 80 meaning the market is overbought ready to drop. It will be interesting to compare the Put ATM Long with the Combo Long Put/Short Call during the March 05 correction where the OEX suffered a drop of more than 16 points in 10 trading days during the Mar 05 option month. Please note that the WWI signaled the drop, rising to greater than 80 on 7th Mar 05. This time let's examine a slightly different strategy than used for the Combo Long Put/Short Call spread:

1. Leave the Credit Short Spread open, allow to expire worthless
2. Open an ATM Long Put 585 with the OEX closing at that date = 584.43

The computations below show the Cost to Open and Value at Expiration for 10 Spreads is given below:

- C590/595   Call Prem = 0.5,   Initial Credit = $426
- P560/555   Put Prem = 0.65, Initial Credit = $ 576
-                    Margin for Condor = 10*5*100 = $5,000
-                    Total Initial Credit for Condor = $1,002
-                    %Return on Margin = 1002/5000 = 20.00%

The Computation for opening 10 ATM Long OEX P585 on   7 Mar 06 and closing the 10 OEX P585 on 18 Mar 06, for a period of 11 days, is given below

- P585 Prem on opening = 4.4, Buy 10 Longs = $4,047
- P585 Prem on closing = 19.4, Sell 10 Longs = $19,326
-                                 Profit for 11 Days = $15,186
-                    % Return on Initial $4,047 Investment = 375.2%

As may be seen, the results of this example of an ATM long Put signaled by the WWI being greater than 80: shows that a profit greater than $15,000 was achieved when the trader used the WWI signal to trade.

In summary we have seen two different strategies to profit OEX Options:

1. Opening ten 2 sigma OEX Condors at the beginning of the Option Month and allowing both sides of the Condor to expire worthless, thus leaving the Initial Credit as the profit.
2. Using WWI>80 to trigger Buying 10 ATM Long Puts and selling after a little more than a week of being open to realize a $15 thousand profit on a modest $4 thousand   investment.   This example shows the large leverage you have on your own trading capital.

OEX Leaps – Long Term Options

A new type index option based on the OEX, called OEX LEAPS, was first placed on the market in January 1991. The CBOE website:

http://www.cboe.com/DelayedQuote/QuoteTable.aspx

The OEX LEAPS expirations: Dec 06 and Dec 07 are shown in the Figure 4.6 below for the next two years, copied from the CBOE website in early Dec 05. Thus OEX LEAPS options are maintained for 2 years. The LEAPS is simply a long term option which expires many months in the future instead of having monthly expirations. LEAPS are used by many traders as a hedge against a drop in the stock market. Please note that in Fig 4.6 below the Dec 06 C580 Open Interest (OI) is 2083 with bid = 34.3, ask = 36.1 and the Dec 06 P580 OI is only 425 with bid = 14.8, ask = 28.9.

Then the Dec 06 P440 has OI = 3925 with an bid value = 2.8, ask value = 3.6 and the Dec 06 P500 has OI = 3468 with bid = 7.9, ask = 8.4

So what do the quotes for the Dec 2006 LEAPS mean? It means that the LEAPS 06 traders believe the ATM Calls are worth 35.2 and the Puts, which are 140 below the money, are worth 8.25 to be used as a hedge against a big drop (more than 140 point drop) in the OEX. Figure 4.6 for OEX LEAPS is shown on the next page.

Dr. Jon Schiller

Figure 4.6 OEX LEAPS for 2006 & 2007

FIGURE46OEXLEAPS20067207

05Jun6600(OEYRLE)	0.75pc	0.25	0.65	0	1	05Jun6600(OEYRLE)	0pc		8.53	8.71	0	0
06Dec3200(YOLLFE)	2.49pc	2.567	2.587	0	4	06Dec3200(YOLXFE)	0.35	-0.15	0.25	0.55	30	471
06Dec3600(YOLLJE)	0pc	2.889	22.09	0	0	06Dec3600(YOLXJE)	0.75pc		0.5	1	0	359
06Dec4000(YOLLNE)	0pc	18.16	18.36	0	0	06Dec4000(YOLXNE)	1.5pc		1.3	1.8	0	359
06Dec4200(YOLLPE)	0pc	16.32	16.52	0	0	06Dec4200(YOLXPE)	2.1pc		1.85	2.65	0	315
06Dec4400(YOLLRE)	0pc	14.5	14.7	0	0	06Dec4400(YOLXRE)	3.1pc		2.8	3.6	0	3925
06Dec4600(YOLLLE)	0pc	12.72	12.92	0	0	06Dec4600(YOLXLE)	4pc		4	4.8	0	1339
06Dec4800(YOLLVE)	0pc	10.97	11.17	0	0	06Dec4800(YOLXVE)	6pc		5.7	6.7	0	963
06Dec5000(YOLLXE)	10.05pc	9.27	9.47	0	6	06Dec5000(YOLXXE)	8pc		7.9	8.4	0	3468
06Dec5200(YOLLZE)	7.0pc	7.65	7.85	0	3	06Dec5200(YOLXZE)	11.2	-0.3	11	11.5	10	594
06Dec5400(YOLLBE)	6.7pc	6.11	6.31	0	2.9	06Dec5400(YOLXBE)	15.7	1.8	14.8	16.2	10	396
06Dec5600(YOLLDE)	5.0pc	4.76	4.89	0	11.2	06Dec5600(YOLXDE)	2.0pc		2.0	21.8	0	218
06Dec5800(YOLLGE)	3.92pc	3.43	3.61	0	2.83	06Dec5800(YOLXGE)	27.5pc		27.1	28.9	0	425
06Dec6000(YOLLIE)	2.91pc	2.41	2.54	0	101	06Dec6000(YOLXIE)	34.9pc		36.7	38.5	0	30
06Dec6200(YOLLKE)	1.6pc	1.5	1.64	0	46.5	06Dec6200(YOLXKE)	62.1pc		49.2	51.2	0	1
06Dec6600(YOLLOE)	0.64pc	0.44	0.52	0	16.6	06Dec6600(YOLXOE)	90.5pc		8.53	87.3	0	3
06Dec7000(YOLLSE)	1.65pc	0.7	1.2	0	7.92	06Dec7000(YOLXSE)	16.89pc		12.53	127.3	0	0
07Dec4000(YOPLNE)	17.2pc	19.02	19.22	0	4.80	07Dec4000(YOPXNE)	53pc		49	59	0	519
07Dec4200(YOPLPE)	0pc	17.35	17.55	0	0.07	07Dec4200(YOPXPE)	68pc		65	75	0	2
07Dec4400(YOPLRE)	0pc	15.72	15.92	0	0.07	07Dec4400(YOPXRE)	13pc		84	94	0	17
07Dec4600(YOPLLE)	0pc	14.12	14.32	0	0.07	07Dec4600(YOPXLE)	11.2pc		10.5	11.9	0	215
07Dec4800(YOPLVE)	0pc	12.57	12.77	0	0.07	07Dec4800(YOPXVE)	14.2pc		13.3	14.7	0	439
07Dec5000(YOPLXE)	10.1pc	11.06	11.26	0	0.07	07Dec5000(YOPXXE)	17.2pc		16.6	18	0	215
07Dec5200(YOPLZE)	8.36pc	9.6	9.8	0	1	07Dec5200(YOPXZE)	25.4pc		20.5	22.3	0	32
07Dec5400(YOPLBE)	8.95pc	8.22	8.42	0	26	07Dec5400(YOPXBE)	26pc		25.3	26	0	157.2
07Dec5600(YOPLDE)	7.65pc	6.91	7.11	0	78	07Dec5600(YOPXDE)	30pc		31.3	33.1	0	152
07Dec5800(YOPLGE)	5.83pc	5.7	5.9	0	16.6	07Dec5800(YOPXGE)	40.2pc		39.4	40.2	0	16.6
07Dec6000(YOPLIE)	5.28pc	4.59	4.79	0	25.0	07Dec6000(YOPXIE)	46pc		47.1	49.1	0	200
07Dec6200(YOPLKE)	4.08pc	3.52	3.8	0	105	07Dec6200(YOPXKE)	0pc		57.5	59.5	0	0
07Dec6600(YOPLOE)	2.32pc	2.05	2.23	0	119	07Dec6600(YOPXOE)	0pc		86.4	88.4	0	0
07Dec7000(YOPLSE)	8.3pc	1.0	1.14	0	620	07Dec7000(YOPXSE)	0pc		12.52	127.2	0	0
07Dec7400(YOPLWE)	5.1pc	4.2	5	0	712	07Dec7400(YOPXWE)	18.2pc		16.52	16.72	0	57
07Dec7400(YOPLWE)	5.1pc	4.2	5	0	712	07Dec7400(YOPXWE)	18.2pc		16.52	16.72	0	57

The Call short credit spread strategy used for Dec 06 OEX LEAPS based upon a short C660/Long C700 would yield an initial credit = 6.4-1.65 = 4.75 points but require a margin of 40 points. For example if a 10 options spread were opened, the Initial Credit = \$4,750 , Margin = 40*10*100 = \$40,000 yielding a return on margin = 11.875% per annum. If the OEX rose less than 90 points during the year 2005 to 2006, this LEAPS trade would be safe and the Initial Credit would become the profit = \$4,750.

Using a Dec 06 LEAPS Put short spread of short Put 460/Long P440 would yield a premium difference = 3.1 – 2.1 = 1.0 points, for a margin = 20 points. For an example of a 10 options spread, the Initial Credit = \$1,000, Margin = 20*10*100 = \$20,000 yielding a return on margin = 1000/20000 = 5.00% per annum. If the OEX remained above 460 for the year from Dec 05 thru Dec 06 expiration, then this LEAPS Put Covered Short Spread would be safe.

I do note that in Dec 2005 there is a lot more OEX LEAPS trading action than during mid 1994 when LEAPS were first introduced into the market. Also the LEAPS have evolved over the last decade to become more similar to Options in terms of strike prices and option premiums. For example, in the beginning of LEAPS, the OEX LEAPS index was one tenth that of the OEX. By 2005 the OEX LEAPS and OEX are the same value – no difference between OEX and OEX LEAPS.

An investment strategy to use for OEX LEAPS is to buy long Put Leaps or long Call Leaps. If you believe the market will rise during the next year, then buy Call Leaps. If you believe the market will drop during the next year, then buy Put Leaps. The market indicators such as MAD4, MADC, and WWI give market signals telling when to buy Call LEAPS, or buy Put LEAPS. *LEAPS gives you a leveraged way to invest in long term bull or bear markets.* For example, if you had believed, confirmed by your market indicators, that the market was going to rise from the Dec 05 to the next Dec 06 LEAPS expiration, then you would have bought 10 Dec 06 Call 660 at premium = 4.6. Cost = 4.60*10*100 = $4,600 plus comm.

How would this strategy profit? Figure 4.7 shows how 10 OEX LEAPS purchased in Dec 05 would profit at expiration on Dec 06 for different values of OEX at expiration. The actual OEX = 666 at expiration 15 Dec 06, so the year investment would have a profit $1225 or a return on investment = 25.6%, still better than many investment funds.

Figure 4.7	short C660/Long C700				40
Date	NOPS	Prem	OEX	Opt Value	Margin
Dec-05	10	4.75	660	-$4,775	$40,000
Dec-06		1.25	666	$1,225	3.06%
Dec-06		35.25	700	$35,225	88.06%
Dec-06		60.25	725	$60,225	150.56%

Please note that this LEAPS Call investment would have lost the original cost, if the OEX had finished less than the Call strike price of 660 at Dec 06 expiration. The profit is shown for 3 examples of the OEX finishing above 660: at 666, (the actual finish OEX value), 700, and 725. The profit grows from $1,225 through over $60,225 for a value of 725 at Dec 06 expiration. To make this large profit, it would have required the OEX to rise 145 points in the 12 months, or an average of 12 points per month. Or, to make a modest $1225, the OEX would have had to rise 86 points or an average of 7.2 points per month to finish at 666.

Now let's examine the economics of investing in two year out OEX LEAPS, buying Calls using the Dec 07 LEAPS. In Dec 05 the Dec 07 OEX LEAPS Call 700 had a premium = 8.3 meaning the cost of 10 OEX LEAPS C700 = 10*100*8.5 = $8,500 plus commission. The profit results of this 2 year out Investment Strategy is shown in Figure 4.8 below. Again in this figure, the possible profits for various values of OEX at expiration on Dec 07 are shown. The actual OEX Dec 07 expiration = 693.57

Figure 4.8	Long Call		700		
Date	NOPS	Prem	OEX	Opt Value	
Dec-05	10	7.3	660	-$7,325	
Dec-07		-41.3	666	-$41,350	-564.51%
Dec-07		-7.3	700	-$7,350	-100.34%
Dec-07		0.2	708	$150	2.05%
Dec-07		17.7	725	$17,650	240.96%
Dec-07		42.7	750	$42,650	582.25%

Please note that for this longer term investment almost all of the total cost of $7,325 would been lost, since the OEX expired at less than 700. At 708, would have been about break-even, and a profit of $42.65 thousand would have been earned, if the OEX finished at 750 or some 175 points above the OEX value when opened in Dec 05. This would have required an average rise of 7.3 points per month for the 24 months from Dec 05 when the Dec 07 LEAPS OEX position was opened. So 2 years leaps are more risky.

Now let's assume you had been a bear or would like to hedge other stock market investments against a market collapse during the next year, how would Put LEAPS fare? A big drop in the OEX during the next year from Dec 05 to Dec 06 would be to drop 75 points to 500. A hedge to profit from such a drop using 10 Dec 06 OEX LEAPS would have been to buy 10 Puts at premium 1.5, cost = 10*100*1.5 = $1,500 + commission. Figure 4.9 below shows the results for different values of OEX at expiration on Dec 06 for the LEAPS

Please note that if the OEX finished at expiration Dec 06 any value above 500, the total hedge investment of $1.525 thousand would have been lost. As may be seen for OEX values at lower than 495, then a profit would have been realized reaching $44.65 thousand at 450. This profit would have been $3,727 per month, but would have required a drop of 150 points or some 12.5 points per month.

Next we examine using two year out LEAPS as a hedge against a major collapse in the market over the next two years from Dec 05 thru Dec 07, Figure 4.10 below shows the results of using the longer out OEX LEAPS:

Figure 4.10 Long Put			500	
Date	NOPS	Prem	OEX	Opt Value
Dec-05	10	5.3	500	-$5,325
Dec-07		5	495	-$350
Dec-07		25	475	$19,650
Dec-07		50	450	$44,650

This shows that a Put 500 strike price LEAPS hedge would cost $5.3 thousand to open the 10 Long Puts and if the OEX finished above 500 on Dec 07 expiration then the total amount of the hedge investment would be lost. It would take a major market collapse to make a large profit. At a collapse to 450 the profit would be $44.6 thousand or some $1,858 per month. **But since the OEX finished at 693.57, you would lost your initial investment of $5.3K**

In summary the use of OEX LEAPS is a way to make good profits for rising markets by buying Long OEX LEAPS one or two years out and a way to make big profits when there is a big drop in the market during the next one or two years. How did the years OEX Dec 2003 to Dec 2005 fare?   OEX Dec 03 = 540, Dec 04 = 567, Dec 05 = 575 for a 1 year delta = 27, a 2 year delta = 35. So you see, 1 or 2 year Call Leaps would have done well if opened in Dec 2003.

For 3 years of Jun expirations::
- Jun 06 expiration OEX = 572
- Jun 07 expiration OEX = 704   Del = +132

- Jun 08 expiration OEX = 572   Del = -107

So you see OEX Long Call leaps would have well between 2006 to 2007, when there was a major Up Trend of 11 points per month. OEX Long Put leaps would have done well between 2007 and 2008, when there was a major Down Trend of 8.9 points per month. But the 2 year Jun leaps were about break even.

OEX Leaps Investment Example in Early 1990's

If you had taken a Long Call position on OEX LEAPS by buying Calls at Strike Price 30, (Dec 92 expiration) in January 1991 when they first came on the market, by Jan 1992 you would have made an annual return of 152.5%; if you had held the Calls until June 92, your return would have fallen to 96.3% per annum. The spectacular success of the OEX LEAPS Dec 92 C30 resulted from the bull leg at the end of the Gulf War in Feb 91 and the huge jump in Jan 92 caused by the Fed's Interest Rate cut at the end of 91. In this chapter you have seen some impressive results of using the later evolution of OEX LEAPS in the year 2005, 2006, and 2007. So you may see the LEAPS strategy can still be profitable when there are large annual rises or drops in the market.

Decision Charts for Long Positions

This chapter has shown how well the two market indicators MADC, MAD and WWI predicted the large changes in the OEX of 2005. The author also observed that the MADC & MAD were good indicators for the Spring 94 Correction that begin in March 94 and ended in May94:

The 100 day MAD signaled the beginning of the downward correction when it turned negative on 24 March 94 and turned even more negative on the 25th. The MADC warned of the down a few days earlier, but it's signal was not as dramatic a warning as the MAD. The MAD turned positive on the 19th May 94 and then moved further into positive territory on the 25th May.

The MADC, meanwhile, remained negative even though the recovery was well under way. So you can see that using the various signal indicators can be confusing and give conflicting signals when a downward correction begins *or* when the recovery from the drop begins. In my experience the MAD is the most reliable and the easiest to compute. My more recent experience with the Welles-Wilder Indicator, WWI > 80, signaling a drop is coming and the WWI <20 signaling a rise is coming is a reliable way of triggering Long Positions.:

- WWI > 80, open an ATM Put to profit from an impending drop
- WWI < 20, open an ATM Call to profit from an impending rise

Algorithms for Computing the MADC

The MADC uses three exponential smoothing factors based upon the number of days for the exponential moving average computations. The number days of smoothing are ND1, ND2, and ND3. ND1 = 2*ND2 and MD3 = ND2*2/3. MADC is always computed using these ratios among the three factors, ND1, ND2, and ND3. The exponential moving average smoothing factors are:

SF1 = 2/(ND1+1), SF2 = 2/(ND2+1), SF3 = 2/(ND3+1)

The three exponential moving averages are computed as follows:

MA1 (i) = SF1*OEX (i) + (1-SF1)*MA1 (i − 1)
MA2 (i) = SF2*OEX (i) + (1-SF2)*MA2 (i − 1)
MA3 (i) = SF3*OEX (i) + (1-SF3)*MA3 (i − 1)
For example if ND1 = 200, then SF1 = 2/(200+1) = 0.0100

If ND1 (i-1) = 424.07, and OEX(i) = 426.23, then MA1(i) = 426.23*0.1+424.07*0.99 = 424.09. Next the difference between MA1 and MA2 are taken for each day;

del(i) = MA2(i) − MA1(i), then the moving average difference is computed using ND3:

MAdel(i) = SF3*delMA(i) + (1-SF3)*MAdel (1-i)
Finally, MADC(i) = delMA(i) − MAdel(i)

It all appears complicated, but is really quite simple when using an Excel spread sheet.

Algorithms for Computing the MAD

The MAD uses a single exponential smoothing factor based on the number of days for the exponential moving average computation. The number of days is ND4.

$$SF4 = 2/(ND4+1)$$

The exponential moving average is computed as follows:

$$MA(i) = SF4*OEX(i) + (1-SF4)*MA(i - 1)$$

For example if ND4 =50, then SF4 = 2/(50 + 1) = .0392

If MA(i - 1) = 424.07, and OEX (i) = 426.23, then

$$MA1(i) = 426.23*0.0392 + 424.07*(0.9608) = 424.15$$

Again an Excel spread sheet makes the computation simple for the trader. Also if you buy my program SelfAdapDTN4 trading software for $70.

Also I include FREE, the program SelfAdapSigIndicOEX which has all the computations and charts and the program also includes a Neural Network combining the signal indicators MAD4, MAD9-4, MADC, and Stochastics %K-%D combined in a 3 layer neural network to shows UP & DOWN market trends, a skill I learned at a Caltech lecture on the subject.

OEX Combo Spread Switch Example in 1994

If you had taken an OEX short naked credit spread position during the April 94 Option month, by March 25th both the MAD & MADC indicators would have told you something was seriously wrong with the market in the downward direction and you had better do something quickly because your short C440/ short P430 was in the money on the Put side. This double warning from the indicators and the fact that your Put short Put was in the money, should have made you take immediate defensive action. The MAD decision chart signaled a serious drop in the market was underway and a switch to a Combo spread would be profitable if the market continued its plunge. The decision charts showed a big drop on 25 March when the moving average difference dropped below 10, which was the support level. This was the definitive signal to make the change from the threatened Put Credit Covered Spread to Long Put/Short Call Combo Spread. We now were shown by the MAD chart the benign market fluctuations of the last 6 or 7 months were over and a was necessary to conserve your capital and make some extra from the big drop. *How to make this switch?*

1. Close out the April naked short spread: C440/ P430 for a cost = 7.6875*10*100+Comm = $7,875 – Naked Spread Initial Credit = $7875 - $6415 = net cost = - $1,460.
2. Open a new Combo Spread: Long Put 420/ Short Call 430, 2.375- 2.875 = 0.5 points, cost of Combo Spread = 0.5*10*100 – Comm = - $600.

So how much did this switch cost? = Close out naked Spread + Cost or Combo Spread = -1460-600 = - $2,060

Did this Switch make money for the April 1994 Option Month?

- On April Expiration: Fri 15 Apr 94, OEX = 411.31
- The Long P 420 = 420 – 411.31 = 8.69 points. Value = 8.69*10*100 = $8,690, the short Call 430 was worthless, so the Combo Spread value = $8,690.
- The *Net Profit for the Apr OpMo* = Value of Combo Spread – Cost of Switch Over from Naked Spread to Combo Spread: $8,690 - $2,060 = *$6,630*

In summary Chart Signal Indicators triggered the close out of the naked short spread and opening of a new Long Put, Short Call Combo Spread that converted a potential big loss into a trading profit for the option month. So you should place the conversion of threatened Short Spreads into Combo Spreads into your bag of tricks to make profits during option months with greater than 2 sigma movements of the OEX.

It is handy to have a reference for the Option Signals which have the first symbol be the month symbol for Calls & Puts. And the second symbol be the symbol for the strike price. The strike price symbol is particularly confusing because there are different symbols for whole number strike prices and those with ½ points.

Figure 4.12 OPTION CODES

Expiration Month Codes [View Option Expiration Calendar]

	JAN	FEB	MAR	APR	MAY	JUN	JUL	AUG	SEP	OCT	NOV	D
Calls	A	B	C	D	E	F	G	H	I	J	K	
Puts	M	N	O	P	Q	R	S	T	U	V	W	

Strike Price Codes

Code		Strike	Prices				Code		Strike	Prices			
A	5	105	205	305	405	505	N	70	170	270	370	470	5
B	10	110	210	310	410	510	O	75	175	275	375	475	5
C	15	115	215	315	415	515	P	80	180	280	380	480	58
D	20	120	220	320	420	520	Q	85	185	285	385	485	5
E	25	125	225	325	425	525	R	90	190	290	390	490	5
F	30	130	230	330	430	530	S	95	195	295	395	495	5
G	35	135	235	335	435	535	T	100	200	300	400	500	6
H	40	140	240	340	440	540	U	7.5	37.5	67.5	97.5	127.5	15
I	45	145	245	345	445	545	V	12.5	42.5	72.5	102.5	132.5	16
J	50	150	250	350	450	550	W	17.5	47.5	77.5	107.5	137.5	16
K	55	155	255	355	455	555	X	22.5	52.5	82.5	112.5	142.5	17
L	60	160	260	360	460	560	Y	27.5	57.5	87.5	117.5	147.5	17
M	65	165	265	365	465	565	Z	32.5	62.5	92.5	122.5	152.5	18

OEX Week Long Options
Weekly Options Open on One Friday, Expire the Following Friday

On 28 October 2005 CBOE Introduced new **Weeklys**. These short term options are based on the S&P 500 Index (SPX) and the S&P 100 Index (OEX). Please note the OEX Weekly options have both American Style – RZB codes, and European Style – KFB codes. Also note the 3rd letter denotes which week.

Weeklys are listed on Mondays and expire the following Friday, as opposed to traditional options which have a life of 4 or 5 weeks or for LEAPS with a life 1 or 2 years. There are, of course, the intermediate life options which have a life of up to 6 months.

Because of the short duration of Weekly contracts, they help traders to trade around specific news or events. The Naked Calls and Naked Puts have the same margin algorithm as for the monthly options whose algorithms were given in Chapter 1.

Weeklys trade use the following symbols: **Figure 4.13**

Figure 4.13a

Calls	Last Sale	Net	Bid	Ask	Vol
08 Jan 680.00 (RZA AP-E)	3.5	-4	3.7	4.2	502
08 Jan 685.00 (RZA AQ-E)	1.7	-5.5	1.75	1.95	201
08 Jan 690.00 (RZA AR-E)	0.6	-4.7	0.6	0.85	565
08 Jan 695.00 (RZA AS-E)	0.25	-1.55	0.15	0.3	149
08 Jan 700.00 (RZA AT-E)	0.15	-0.7	0.05	0.25	75
08 Jan 705.00 (RZA AA-E)	0.05	-0.55	0	0.2	33
08 Jan 710.00 (RZA AB-E)	0.05	-0.1	0.05	0.1	250

Figure 4.13b

Puts	Last Sale	Net	Bid	Ask	Vol
08 Jan 680.00 (RZA MP-E)	6.3	2.4	5.7	6.6	143
08 Jan 685.00 (RZA MQ-E)	11	6.1	8.6	9.6	16
08 Jan 690.00 (RZA MR-E)	14	7	13.3	14	17
08 Jan 695.00 (RZA MS-E)	9	0	18.2	19.7	0
08 Jan 700.00 (RZA MT-E)	11.4	0	23	24.8	0
08 Jan 705.00 (RZA MA-E)	0	0	28	29.8	0
08 Jan 710.00 (RZA MB-E)	0	0	33	34.8	0

Weeklys OEX options are to be added to our bag of strategies. See OEX Weekly CCSS Computations below as **Figure 4.14**. As you may see the % Return on Margin ranges from 8.6% to 28.6% for OEX spreads.   You can lose for large market movements, for example on Tue 24 Jun 08, I opened 5 Put Spreads at 1.4 the next day the OEX plunged and I had to close out at 4.4, a big loss.   This was the week of an 18 point drop on Thursday, follow by a 3.76 point drop Friday.

I now have a new rule: **Don't open OEX weekly option until Thu or Fri, to reduce the risk of the weekly spread strategy.** By waiting late in the week you have a higher probability of making a good profit. An example of OEX weekly spread: Opened 5 Weekly short C585 long C590 for which I received a premium of 0.6, Initial Credit = 0.6*5*100-commission 15.5 = $284. Since the OEX finished below 585, the initial credit became profit at market close that Friday. Good profit for a one day trade. Note: since it was a spread, the day-trader rules did not apply.

Figure 4.14

OEX WEEKLYS	NOPS=	5	Comm=	3.5	574.01	
Calls	Last Sale	Net	Bid	Ask	Vol	Open Int
05 Dec 570.0 (RZE LN-E)	8.4 –		5.4	6.4	20	0
05 Dec 575.0 (RZE LO-E)	2.3	-4.4	2.2	2.4	33	0
05 Dec 580.0 (RZE LP-E)	0.65	-2.2	0.6	0.75	755	135
05 Dec 585.0 (RZE LQ-E)	0.15	-0.5	0.1	0.2	826	338
05 Dec 590.0 (RZE LR-E)	0.15	-0.05	0	0.1	647	22
sC580/L585 =	0.50	$215	Initial Credit			
Margin =	$2,500					
%Ret =	8.60%					

27-Dec-05

Puts	Last Sale	Net	Bid	Ask	Vol	Open Int
05 Dec 570.0 (RZE XN-E)	1.2	0.6	0.95	1.3	660	21
05 Dec 575.0 (RZE XO-E)	2.7	1.3	2.7	3.2	745	343
05 Dec 580.0 (RZE XP-E)	5.3	2.35	5.7	6.7	79	31
05 Dec 585.0 (RZE XQ-E)	9	2.5	10.2	11.4	2	2
05 Dec 590.0 (RZE XR-E)	12.9 –		15.2	16.4	20	0
sP575/L570 =	1.50	$715	Initial Credit			
Margin =	$2,500					
%Ret =	28.60%					

Part 1 Options Trading Strategy for Capital Growth

Chapter 5 Capital Growth Prediction

It is important to keep track of your capital growth. The growth of your capital depends upon how much option trading collateral you start with, how much trading profit you realize at each month's option expiration, how much you have withdrawn from your monthly profits and how you invest your capital with your broker. You should remember that for most capital investments used for collateral your broker will only allow 80% - and for some Mutual Funds only 50% - to be used for Trading Margin. Please Note: TradeKing provides a list of Mutual Funds that can be traded in their Options Accounts, some of which allowed 100% of their value to applied to Margin, so the number of options used in the examples below are pessimistic.

We will use two investment allocations. Let us assume that the beginning capital is $25,000. The allocations are below:

1. Mutual Funds 50%, Growth Stocks 10%, Money Market 40%
2. Mutual Funds 25%, Growth Stocks 50%, Money Market 25%

Assume the annual growth rate for the Investments are below:

- Mutual Funds = 60% per annum
- Growth Stocks = 50% per annum
- Money Market = 4% per annum

Let us assume that we use half of the available margin for making the Covered Credit Short Spreads (CCSS). As the capital grows, then the number of options traded in the CCSS's are increased.

My Excel Workbook: SelfAdapDTN4.xls has an Excel Worksheet: SelfAdapCapitGrwth with a model for showing Capital Growth from option trading. You may use this worksheet for keeping track of your actual capital and its growth using the model for the algorithms needed.. I have included the parameters I have found to be approximate to use as default values. You may modify the parameters to suit your own case to make the capital growth meet your particular case. The nice thing about Excel

Workbooks, is the worksheets allow the particularization to me or you to be made quite simply.

The Excel Workbook: SelfAdapDTN4.xls is described in Chapter 6. This workbook is used for keeping track of your daily trading and has a work sheet for OEX, SPX, 18 Growth Stocks, and one Mutual Fund with charts for each of these indices, stocks, and fund. In addition I have added recently to this Workbook sheets for tracking QLD and QID, to special stocks used by http://www.disciplined-qqq-trading.com/ which issues a daily email newsletter advisory telling when to buy and sell QLD & QID. I use it with TradeKing AutoTrade service, but you can do the trading manually, if you are not a TradeKing client. The work sheets also compute the WWI for the indices, and most of the stocks and funds. The results of the capital growth using 2 sigma CCSS using capital allocations 1 & 2 are described in this chapter. Chapter 6 describes the algorithms used in these two spread sheets with hints on how you can customize the worksheet to keep track of your own monthly trading results as well as your personal Capital Allocation.

A spread sheet from SelfAdapDTN4.xls using allocation 1 is shown in Figure 5.1 below. Starting with $ 25,000 at the beginning of the first year using the parameters of the spread sheet the Capital has grown to $33,793 and the # of options has grown from 10 to 17 with the monthly income from $1,078 the 1st month to $2,274 at the 12th month.

Your actual results may be better or worse.

Figure 5.1 Simulated Capital Growth Allocation 1

Effective 20 Jun 08   **Trade Model begins with $ $20,000**

	Broker Acct			One point Loss Once/Year			Conservative Model Parameters		
	CAPITAL	NOPS	PRM	INIT CRDT	MARGN	PRFT	CUM PRFT	%Ret Mgn	%Ret Cap
Jul-08	$25,000	13	1.1	$1,404	$13,000	$1,404	$1,404	10.80%	5.62%
Aug-08	$26,404	13	1.1	$1,404	$13,000	$1,404	$2,808	10.80%	5.32%
Sep-08	$27,808	14	1.1	$1,513	$14,000	$1,513	$4,321	10.81%	5.44%
Oct-08	$29,321	15	1.1	$1,622	$15,000	$1,622	$5,943	10.81%	5.53%
Nov-08	$30,943	15	1.1	$1,622	$15,000	$1,622	$7,564	10.81%	5.24%
Dec-08	$32,564	16	-1	-$1,630	$16,000	-$1,630	$5,934	-10.19%	-5.00%
Jan-09	$30,934	15	1.1	$1,622	$15,000	$1,622	$7,556	10.81%	5.24%
Feb-09	$32,556	16	1.1	$1,730	$16,000	$1,730	$9,286	10.81%	5.31%
Mar-09	$34,286	17	1.1	$1,839	$17,000	$1,839	$11,125	10.82%	5.36%
Apr-09	$36,125	18	1.1	$1,948	$18,000	$1,948	$13,072	10.82%	5.39%
May-09	$38,072	19	1.1	$2,056	$19,000	$2,056	$15,129	10.82%	5.40%
Jun-09	$40,129	20	1.1	$2,165	$20,000	$2,165	$17,294	10.83%	5.40%
Jul-09	$42,294	21	1.1	$2,274	$21,000	$2,274	$19,567	10.83%	5.38%

To compare the capital growth using the capital allocation 2 please see Figure 5.2 below:

Starting with $ 25,000 at the beginning of the first year using the parameters of the spread sheet the Capital has grown to $60,986 and the # of options has grown from 10 to 25 and the monthly income from has grown from $2,343 the 1st month to $4.759 at the 12th month.

Starting with $60,986 at the end of the first year using the parameters of the spread sheet the Capital has grown to $197,223 and the # of options has grown from 28 to 140 and the monthly income from $7,337 the 13th month to $23,714 at the 24th month.

By comparing Figure 5.1 and Figure 5.2, you may see that the results are almost the same with the allocation 2 making (197,223-181963)/25,000 =61% more above the beginning $25,000 capital. So you may adjust your parameters to suit you personal desires and you will probably do well using 2 sigma CCSS for the monthly income and Long Calls and Puts triggered by WWI for the extra income. I used a loss of 2 points once per year when the OEX moves greater than 2 sigma up or down. This is a reasonable loss rate. However, one may never predict exactly what will happen.

Please Go to the Next Page to See Capital Growth Using Allocations 1 &2 in Figure 5.2

Figure 5.2 Simulated Capital Growth with Allocation 2

Simulated Capital Growth with Investment Allocation 2

Starting Capital =	$25,000		$350					
Type of Investment	CapAlloc	CapAmt	%Gwth/yr	Pft/Yr	Pft/Mo	Margn%	AmtMgn	Mgn/CCSS
Mutual Funds	25%	$6,250	60%	$3,750	$313	50%	$3,125	$1,000
Growth Stocks	50%	$12,500	50%	$6,250	$521	80%	$10,000	
Money Market	25%	$6,250	4%	$250	$21	100%	$6,250	
Total =	100%	$25,000	41.0%	$10,250	$854		$19,375	10

Date	NCPS	GrPPrm	InitOrd	LrgPrm	LrgPft#	LrgPft	InvPftM	AppCapit	TotCap
Jan06	10	1.20	$1,074	0.9	5	$415	$854	$10,859	$27,343
Feb06	11	1.20	$1,243	0.9	6	$498	$854	$12,156	$29,938
Mar06	12	1.20	$1,356	0.9	6	$498	$854	$13,511	$32,646
Apr06	14	1.20	$1,582	0.9	7	$581	$854	$15,019	$35,663
May06	15	1.20	$1,695	0.9	8	$664	$854	$16,626	$38,876
Jun06	17	(2.00)	($3,519)	0.9	9	$747	$854	$15,667	$36,959
Jul06	16	1.20	$1,808	0.9	8	$664	$854	$17,330	$40,285
Aug06	17	1.20	$1,921	0.9	9	$747	$854	$19,091	$43,807
Sep06	19	1.20	$2,147	0.9	10	$830	$854	$21,007	$47,638
Oct06	21	1.20	$2,373	0.9	11	$913	$854	$23,077	$51,778
Nov06	23	1.20	$2,599	0.9	12	$996	$854	$25,301	$56,227
Dec06	25	1.20	$2,825	0.9	13	$1,079	$854	$27,680	$60,986

$60,986	$60,986							
	25%	$15,246	60%	$9,148	$762	50%	$7,623	$1,000
	50%	$30,493	50%	$15,246	$1,271	80%	$24,394	
	25%	$15,246	4%	$610	$51	100%	$15,246	
Total =	100%	$60,986	41.0%	$25,004	$2,084		$47,264	24

Jan07	28	1.20	$3,164	0.9	14	$1,162	$2,084	$34,090	$67,395
Feb07	34	1.20	$3,842	0.9	17	$1,411	$2,084	$41,427	$74,732
Mar07	41	1.20	$4,633	0.9	21	$1,743	$2,084	$49,866	$83,192
Apr07	50	1.20	$5,650	0.9	25	$2,075	$2,084	$59,695	$93,000
May07	60	1.20	$6,780	0.9	30	$2,490	$2,084	$71,049	$104,354
Jun07	71	(2.00)	($14,697)	0.9	36	$2,988	$2,084	$61,423	$94,729
Jul07	61	1.20	$6,893	0.9	31	$2,573	$2,084	$72,973	$106,278
Aug07	73	1.20	$8,249	0.9	37	$3,071	$2,084	$86,377	$119,682
Sep07	86	1.20	$9,718	0.9	43	$3,569	$2,084	$101,747	$135,053
Oct07	102	1.20	$11,526	0.9	51	$4,233	$2,084	$119,590	$152,895
Nov07	120	1.20	$13,560	0.9	60	$4,980	$2,084	$140,214	$173,519
Dec07	140	1.20	$15,820	0.9	70	$5,810	$2,084	$163,927	$197,233

I have extended the Capital Growth predictions for two more years using the same parameters for both the allocation 1 and the allocation 2 cases. Please find Figure 5.3a for the next two years for Investment Allocation 1 in the chart below:

Please note in Fig 5.3a that at the end of the 3rd year the capital has grown to $775,075 and the monthly income has grown to $104,121. At the end of the 4th year the capital has grown to $3,179,175. So here is an example in which $25,000 has grown to more than $3 million. I must warn you that such good results are NOT guaranteed. Options trading is risky business and you personally may not do nearly as well as this example.

Please note in Fig 5.2a that at the end of the 3rd year the capital has grown to $864,664 and the monthly income has grown to $117,152. At the end of the 4th year the capital has grown to $3,179,135. So here is an example in which $25,000 has grown to more than $3 million. I must warn you that such good results are **NOT** guaranteed. Options trading is risky business and you personally may not do nearly as well as this example.

Figure 5.3b 3rd & 4th Allocation 2, Extended 2 Years below:

Figure 5.3b 3rd & 4th									
		25%	$49,308	60%	$29,585	$2,465	50%	$24,654	$1,000
		50%	$98,616	50%	$49,308	$4,109	80%	$78,893	
		25%	$49,308	4%	$1,972	$164	100%	$49,308	
		100%	$197,233	41.0%	$80,865	$6,739		$152,855	77

Jan-08	164	1.20	$18,532	0.9	82	$6,806	$6,739	$196,004	$229,309
Feb-08	196	1.20	$22,148	0.9	98	$8,134	$6,739	$233,025	$266,330
Mar-08	233	1.20	$26,329	0.9	117	$9,711	$6,739	$275,804	$309,109
Apr-08	276	1.20	$31,188	0.9	138	$11,454	$6,739	$325,184	$358,490
May-08	325	1.20	$36,725	0.9	163	$13,529	$6,739	$382,177	$415,482
Jun-08	382	(2.00)	($79,074)	0.9	191	$15,853	$6,739	$325,695	$359,000
Jul-08	326	1.20	$36,838	0.9	163	$13,529	$6,739	$382,801	$416,106
Aug-08	383	1.20	$43,279	0.9	192	$15,936	$6,739	$448,755	$482,060
Sep-08	449	1.20	$50,737	0.9	225	$18,675	$6,739	$524,905	$558,211
Oct-08	525	1.20	$59,325	0.9	263	$21,829	$6,739	$612,798	$646,103
Nov-08	613	1.20	$69,269	0.9	307	$25,481	$6,739	$714,287	$747,592
Dec-08	714	1.20	$80,682	0.9	357	$29,631	$6,739	$831,339	$864,644

	$864,644	$864,644							
		25%	$49,308	60%	$29,585	$2,465	50%	$24,654	$1,000
		50%	$98,616	50%	$49,308	$4,109	80%	$78,893	
		25%	$49,308	4%	$1,972	$164	100%	$49,308	
		100%	$197,233	41.0%	$80,865	$6,739		$152,855	77

Jan-08	831	1.20	$93,903	0.9	416	$34,528	$6,739	$966,508	$999,814
Feb-08	967	1.20	$109,271	0.9	484	$40,172	$6,739	$1,122,690	$1,155,995
Mar-08	1123	1.20	$126,899	0.9	562	$46,646	$6,739	$1,302,974	$1,336,279
Apr-08	1303	1.20	$147,239	0.9	652	$54,116	$6,739	$1,511,068	$1,544,373
May-08	1511	1.20	$170,743	0.9	756	$62,748	$6,739	$1,751,298	$1,784,603
Jun-08	1751	(2.00)	($362,457)	0.9	876	$72,708	$6,739	$1,468,287	$1,501,593
Jul-08	1468	1.20	$165,884	0.9	734	$60,922	$6,739	$1,701,832	$1,735,137
Aug-08	1702	1.20	$192,326	0.9	851	$70,633	$6,739	$1,971,530	$2,004,835
Sep-08	1972	1.20	$222,836	0.9	986	$81,838	$6,739	$2,282,943	$2,316,248
Oct-08	2283	1.20	$257,979	0.9	1142	$94,786	$6,739	$2,642,446	$2,675,752
Nov-08	2642	1.20	$298,546	0.9	1321	$109,643	$6,739	$3,057,374	$3,090,679
Dec-08	3057	1.20	$345,441	0.9	1529	$126,907	$6,739	$3,536,461	$3,569,766

The Excel worksheet named CapitalGrwthModel is part of the workbook: SelfAdapDTN4 was used in Figure 5.1 above for predicting the capital growth starting with $25,000 capital in Jul 08 for one year until Jul 09, using the 2 sigma OEX double sided Covered Credit Short Spread, or Condor, for generating the monthly income. The profit could be increased by plus using Welles-Wilder Indicator (WWI) for triggering (ATM) Long Calls (WWI<20) and ATM Long Puts (WWI>80) for augmenting the CCSS monthly income. Note that I used a 1 point loss each year to account for unfavorable market movements. You would need to enter into the SelfAdapCapitGrwth spread sheets your personalized parameters to predict your own case of predicted capital growth.

For example you would enter the actual allocation of assets to Mutual Funds, stocks, and money market that you have invested, as well as the percentage of these assets your broker would allow to be used for option trading margin.

I would also recommend that you enter a sheet next to the SelfAdapCapitGrwth worksheet to keep track of your actual trading results. This could be data entered beginning with the first month you start trading and the future months would be the predicted results using your personal parameters. This short study shows that you should avoid the monthly losses by using the techniques for correcting threatened short Calls or Puts described in Chapter 4, such as switch to Combo Spreads of Long Calls or Puts.

Part 2 Spread Sheet Tools for Index Options Trading

Chapter 6 How to Use Excel Spread Sheets

I have found spread sheets as exemplified by Excel as an indispensable tool for index option trading. The amount of data accumulated during the option trading can be overwhelming. Excel spread sheets allow you to dominate this data in a logical and organized way. Charts generated from the spread sheets allow you to visualize the data. The spread sheet software I use is from Microsoft Office 97 which features Excel 97 and also includes Word for word-processing and Power Point for creating slide presentations. Although I have over 376 spread sheets and chart files I have used during the last 20 years of options trading, at the current time I use 4 workbooks for options and currency trading which are named:

- SelfAdapDTN4.xls for the basic Index & stock option trading including a control center sheet for automatically entering real time data from DTN.IQ
- SelfAdapSigIndicOEX.xls for generating all of the signal indicator charts plus a Neural Network sheet

for measuring the OEX market trends: Up or Down, which uses data linked from SeldAdapDTN4.xls

- SelfAdapFutOp.xls for option trading 10 Futures including a spread sheet and chart for each of the futures, which uses futures data from: http://www.orionfutures.com/

- SelfAdapCur.xls for WWI triggered currency trading for 4 currencies and one currency hedge including a currency control center for entering the realtime data from MGforex: http://www.mgforex.com/eng/forex-tools/content/forex-rates.htm

I will describe each of the last 3 of these work books in detail in Chapter 7. However, I will describe in detail the use of SelfAdapDTN4.xls workbook in this chapter, since this is the *workhorse* workbook for trading OEX monthly condors, as well as OEX Weekly Covered Credit Short Spreads and the WWI triggered Long Call and Put trading for 20 technical stocks.

I must confess, my favorite strategy is using OEX double sided Covered Credit Spreads (Condor) with the short Call 2 sig above the market and the short Put 2 sig below the market, which yield a return on Margin allocated   Typical return on Margin for 2 sigma OEX condors is 19%.

My second favorite is using 1 or 2 day trades using QLD & QID buy-sell signals emailed by: http://www.disciplined-qqq-trading.com/ (a service that costs about $40/mo). During mid-2008 months, the Disciplined-QQQ advisories bought a monthly return of 14% capital allocated to this trading. I use TradeKing AutoTrade to do the actual trading, but you can use the emailed advisories to do the trading manually with your broker, if you don't have TradeKing as a broker. Typically using $7000 allocated to this trading, the trades generate about $1000 per month. This is not guaranteed, but what I experienced during Jun & Jul 08.

Excel Spread Sheets (Work Sheets)

An Excel spread sheet (also called a work sheet) shows on your screen as rows and columns, the vertical columns are designated as A, B, C,....... and the horizontal rows are designated 1,2,3,......... Your spread sheet will contain as many rows and columns as needed to perform the data storage and computations for your tasks. The intersection of a row and column is called a cell and is designated as LETTER-NUMBER, for example B3 which is a cell, is the cell at the intersection of Column B and Row 3 in the worksheet. Each cell can contain a number, a calculation, text or can refer to another cell in this worksheet or any other worksheet including worksheets in other workbooks.

The numbers can be formatted in 12 types including numbers, dates, %'s, fractions, times, currency (in dollars or other currencies) and special formats. In other words the spread sheet can be customized to do the tasks required or assigned to the workbook.

Excel includes a large number of mathematical functions including the basic arithmetic functions: + add, - subtract, * multiply, / divide or more complex mathematical functions including: standard deviation, square root, square, exponential, trend prediction, etc. In addition you may create special functions using Macros or use the Add-in Macros furnished with Excel which are furnished with Excel. The use of Macros is described in Excel's user manual, but simply: you turn on the Macro, perform a number of steps using the means for moving about the worksheet, then complete the Macro and assign a way to invoke the Macro such as CtrlA. Then when you wish to perform the Macro, click on CtrlA and the Macro will be actuated and perform it's tasks. The Macros are coded in Visual Basic, so you may modify the macro by using the VB edit. I use a Macro in SelfAdapCur invoked by CtrlX for entering the realtime Currency copied from Mgforex.

I use simple 'paste special, text' to enter data copied from DTN.IQ Watchlist Portfolio in SelfAdapDTN4 which includes, Indices, Stocks, and Options for the Indices & Stocks. This copied/special paste data is used for computing all computations as well as making the realtime updates of the charts.   DTN.IQ also has realtime OEX option chain & Charts for superimposing on the trading center of SelfAdapDTN4 worksheet.

Workhorse Workbook: SELFADAPDTN4.XLS

This section describes the nuts and bolts of how to use the Excel *workhorse* Workbook SelfAdapDTN4.xls in option trading. The principal worksheet of this Workbook is OpCmdCntr. The columns A through J and the rows for the Jan 2006 option month are shown below in Figure **6.1. Option Command Center (OpCmdCntr)**

1

Figure 6.1a

SelfAdapDTN4 Trading Center

SPX 1,239.76	Date	12-Sep-08	ATM Longs	Prm Got	Prm Now	
0.9 573.00	NOPS =	2	C655	11.91	7.80	
OEX Del -5.88	Comm =	$11.60	P655	11.09	5.40	

OEX DTN Options

		TK Cap =	$18,214 Mgn%Cap =		
573.00	-5.88	2Sig 40.02	$39,584 After OEX Trade		
CNDR NOPS = 10	NOPS =	2	OEX/SPX	SPX Del	StkPrice
2SigCall	615 2SigPut	535	0.46	-9.29	43.02

OEX Crdt Spreads

			Total =			
			$981 Condor Expir	QLD		15-Aug-08
P555/565 Wkly	1.35	0.40	$653	$924	$5,000	33.12%
C580/585 Wkly	1.35	0.34	$1,328	$986	$1,656	$1,311
C630/635	0.35	0.00	$328	$326	33.12%	$1,656
C635/640	0.35	0.00	$328	$326	$966	$5,000
P545/540	0.66	0.40	$638	$234	$560	19.12%
C625/630	0.34	0.05	$318	$42	$5,000	

Now to describe the details of the spreadsheet in Figure 6.1 above.

1. Use this spread sheet to keep track of intraday fluctuations in the OEX, stocks, and covered spreads and any open Long Calls or Puts.

2. Keep track of realtime value of Put and Call Premiums and the Unearned profit on Covered Credit Short Spreads and Long Calls and Puts that may be opened. You may also *paper trade* any of these positions if you have not opened the position with your broker.

3.   This workbook computes the 2 sigmas to use in computing the safe Call and Put strike prices for a covered short spread for OEX, SPX, and the several of the 20 technical stocks tracked.

4. The premiums are obtained real time from DTN.IQ (a service that costs about $40/Mo). Separate worksheets are used for entering CBOE 15 minutes delayed for:

- OEX
- SPX
- GOOG
- SPY
- QQQQ and the related QLD & QID
- AAPL
- Or any other Stock or Index you may develop an interest in tracking in detail by merely inserting a new worksheet for the newly interested stock or index. The historical data can be obtained from Yahoo for creating the new stock worksheet.

The CBOE 15 minute delayed quotes are obtained from:

http://www.cboe.com/DelayedQuote/QuoteTable.aspx

The DTN.IQ service can be obtained from the following website:

http://www.dtniq.com/http://www.dtniq.com/

The DTN.IQ realtime Watchlist quotes by subscribing to the DTN.IQ service which costs about $40/month. My software SelfAdapDTN4 is organized to accept these realtime quotes by copying the Watchlist portfolio and ***paste special, text*** on the sheet OpQte2 of my software.

A portion of the portfolio set up for the Aug 08 options trading month is shown below in Figure 6.1b, which shows only 38 rows out of a total of 126 rows. Normally if I have a new interest in options or equities, I edit the DTN.IQ Watch list at the bottom, and then when copied to OpQte2 sheet, I need to pulldown the new rows on the **SelfAdapStkOp4.xls Command Center**

Sheet of SelfAdapDTN4 workbook. Then I can refer to the new rows in any

computations anywhere in the workbook. The Figure 6.1b is shown below.

Please Go to the Next Page to See Figure 6.1b

Figure 6.1b

SelfAdapDTN4 Trading Center

				ATM Longs	Prm Got	Prm Now
	SPX	1,239.76	Date	12-Sep-08		
0.9	573.00	NOPS =	2	C655	11.91	7.80
OEX Del	-5.88	Comm =	$11.60	P655	11.09	5.40

OEX DTN Options

				TK Cap =	$18,214	Mgn%Cap =	
573.00	-5.88	2Sig	40.02		$39,584	After OEX Trade	
CNDR NOPS = 10		NOPS =	2	OEX/SPX		SPX Del	StkPrice
2SigCall	615	2SigPut	535	0.46		-9.29	43.02

OEX Crdt Spreads

		Total =		$981	Condor Expir	QLD	15-Aug-08
P555/565 Wkly	1.35	0.40	$653		$924	$5,000	33.12%
C580/585 Wkly	1.35	0.34	$1,328		$986	$1,656	$1,311
C630/635	0.35	0.00	$328		$326	33.12%	$1,656
C635/640	0.35	0.00	$328		$326	$966	$5,000
P545/540	0.66	0.40	$638		$234	$560	19.12%
C625/630	0.34	0.05	$318		$42	$5,000	
Expir 18 Sep		Total =	$956		$276	19.12%	%Ret/Mn
Jun 2SIG COVERED SPREADS		Today =		12-Sep-08		23.00	$4,623

AAPL DTN Options

			RIO =	23.13		0.24	
Rate	148.00	-4.65	2Sig = 27.39		Prob Safe		72.04
NOPS =	5						
C200/210	0.64	0.00	$305		$296	$5,000	17.28%
P150/145	1.15	2.24	$560		-$570	$864	-0.97%
2SigCall	175	2Sig Put	120				

RIMM DTN Option

			NOPS = 5				
107.74	-1.58	2Sig = 14.48		Prob Safe		67.54%	
NOPS =	5	1			MRI = 88.52		
C125/130	1.00	0.13	$485		$158	$869	
P100/95	0.80	0.72	$385		$0	$2,500	34.76%
2SigCall	120	2SigPut	95				

RIO DTN Options

			C42.5/45			P 37.5/35	
23.13	0.24	2Sig = 2.41					
NOPS =	5		Init Crdt	Prft	Mgn		C42.5/45
C35/36	0.26	0.01	$115	$110	$954		P37.5/35
P30/25	1.71	5.21	$840	-$1,766	$2,500		38.16%
2SigCall	25	2SigPut	20		$954		SPY Del

SPY DTN Options

		Spy Cnd	$426	WWI =	41.94	-1.33
2SigCall	130	2SigPut	118	124.18	(1.33)	
SPY	124.18	2Sig = 5.31				
NOPS = 10		Comm = 22.00		Spy Cndr =	$426	$248
C134/136	0.22	0.00	$198	$204	$2,000	33.68%
P118/116	0.25	0.18	$228	$44	$248	$674

QQQQ DTN Options

			8	107	Prft qqq =	$0
43.02	-0.58	2Sig = 3.25		#Stks	QLD/QID	
NOPS = 10		Comm = 22.00			$65.03	-$1.89
		QQQQ Cndr	$419		48.40	1.48
C48/50	0.25	0.00	$230	$234	$2,000	20.97%
P41/39	0.21	0.11	$190	$84		$419
Call		46	2Sig Put	40		CndCrdt

LDK DTN Options

		NOPS = 5				
42.61	-1.80	2Sig = 7.19		Prob Safe		67.54%
NOPS =	5			-$241		
C45/50	0.50	0.95	$235	-$241	$2,500	18.76%
P30/25	0.50	0.20	$235	$135	$469	
0.14	0.03					
2SigCall	50	2SigPut	35		$235	9.38%

GOOG DTN Options

432.91	-0.84	2Sig = 61.26				
NOPS =	2	Comm = 17.40		3		%Ret/Mn
2SigCall	490	2SigPut	370			
C610/620	0.90	0.00	$168	$168	$317	15.84%
P490/480	0.80	2.30	$148	-$312	$2,000	

DRYS DTN Options

53.40	-1.72	2Sig = 7.18		Prob Safe		67.54%
NOPS =	5					
C85/90	1.15	-	$560	$560	$1,269	
P70/65	1.45	4.60	$710	-$1,591	$2,500	50.76%
2SigCall	60	2SigPut	45			$1,269

BIDU DTN Options

273.75	-8.77	2Sig = 89.35		Prob Safe	67.54%
NOPS =	2	1			%Safe =

Now to describe the details of SelfAdapDTN4 workbook: The worksheet shown in Figure 6.1b above allows you to keep track of the daily fluctuations in the OEX and how it varies relative to your 2 sigma Covered Credit Short Spread (CCSS). This spread sheet also keeps track of the max and min daily and monthly fluctuations of OEX. It uses this data to compute the monthly 2 sigmas – the parameters you need to compute your safe short Call and short Put strike prices for the covered spreads. This spreadsheet computes a number other   parameters as well including: unrealized profit, the collateral required for your spread, and you may view if your short spread has moved from the safe region to the dangerous in-the-money region which may require protective action.

Several decision charts are generated from another workbook (SelfAdapSigIndicOEX.xls) described in Chapter 7 and generated from this other workbook to aid you in visualizing your short spread on a daily basis during the option month.

The workhorse workbook SelfAdapDTN4.xls has a separate worksheet and Charts for most of the following indices and stocks for keeping track of daily fluctuations for the following underlying markets:

1. OEX
2. SPX
3. AAPL
4. RIMM
5. RIO
6. SPY
7. QQQQ
8. QLD
9. QID
10. LDK
11. GOOG
12. ORCL
13. DRYS
14. BIDU
15. CEO
16. NFLX
17. OXY

18. FLATX (a Hi Grwth Mutual Fund)

Each of the sheets for the above 15 stocks and indices computes the following trading parameters for each market:

- Welles-Wilder Indicator (WWI)
- A logical trigger cell to tell when to open a Long Call when WWI<20 including the ATM strike price of the long Call
- A logical trigger cell to tell when to open a Long Put when WWI>80 including the ATM strike price of the long Put
- 3 columns to the right of the trigger columns to compute the cost and profit for any Long Calls or Puts executed
- Seven columns L thru R for computing the 2 Sigma (two standard deviation) for most of the underlying indices and stocks listed above.

Samples for the sheets will be given in Figures 6.3 a ,b ,c and Figure 6.4 below.

Trading Form Spread Sheet for SelfAdapDTN4.xls

A segment of the TradeForm worksheet from SelfAdapDTN4.xls is shown in Fig 6.2 below: This Figure shows the 2 sigma CCSS for OEX and GOOG for the Jan 06 option month. This same worksheet also computes the SPX and SPY 2 sigma CCSS not shown in the figure. It is a particularly useful worksheet to use before opening the positions for the new option month, using the quotes from the CBOE delayed quotes at the end of the day. The quotes for all the Calls and Puts are copied from the DTN.IQ Watchlist and copied into OpQte2 sheet as explained above.

Figure 6.3d below shows a portion of the OEX worksheet:

Date	Symbol OEXXO	Up	Down	Up7daexMa	Dn7daexMa	WW	Cds<20	Pds>80	Cost Long
16-Jun-06	572.76	0.00	-1.41	2.56	-2.03	55.74			
19-Jun-06	568.53	0.00	-4.23	1.92	-2.58	42.65			
20-Jun-06	568.72	0.19	0.00	1.49	-1.94	43.44			
21-Jun-06	573.71	4.99	0.00	2.36	-1.45	61.94			
22-Jun-06	570.82	0.00	-2.89	1.77	-1.81	49.45			
23-Jun-06	569.47	0.00	-1.35	1.33	-1.70	43.93			
26-Jun-06	572.29	2.82	0.00	1.70	-1.27	57.22			

Two Sigma Computations Using SelfAdapStkOp.xls

Figure 6.3e on the next page shows that portion of the OEX worksheet that computes the 2 sigmas for OEX

Figure 6.3e

OEX 2Sigma Covered Credit Spread

Mo	Max	Min	Max-Min
Jul-06	584.74	566.62	18.12
Aug-06	601.50	572.50	29.00
Sep-06	609.01	598.44	10.57
Oct-06	636.01	609.01	27.00
Nov-06	652.60	635.50	17.10
Dec-06	663.11	642.48	20.63
Jan-07	666.03	656.21	9.82
Feb-07	670.21	659.55	10.66
Mar-07	670.05	630.47	39.58
Apr-07	680.82	633.94	46.88
May-07	699.80	677.11	22.69
Jun-07	699.80	685.33	14.47
Jul-07	718.11	687.78	30.33
Aug-07	714.76	655.83	58.93
Sep-07	713.53	668.99	44.54
Oct-07	729.79	700.31	29.48
Nov-07	724.40	670.37	54.03
Dec-07	706.34	657.79	48.55
Jan-08	699.84	620.43	79.41
Feb-08	699.84	612.82	87.02
Mar-08	635.56	589.15	46.41
Apr-08	640.60	610.31	30.29
May-08	653.49	635.57	17.92
Jun-08	653.10	597.13	55.97
Jul-08	601.45	555.99	45.46
Aug-08	604.47	578.67	25.80
101.5%	**6 Mo**	**OEX 2SIG = 29.04**	
176.4%	**3 Mo**	**OEX 2SIG = 30.63**	
Use	**13 Mo**	**OEX 2SIG = 40.02**	

To compare the OEX 2SIG above with the Weekly OEX 2SIG look at Figure 6.3f below:

Fig 6.3f Weekly 2sig

	OEX MAX	OEX MIN	DEL
25-Apr-08	644.85	635.57	9.28
2-May-08	653.47	641.00	12.47
9-May-08	653.49	641.00	12.49
16-May-08	646.03	639.20	6.83
23-May-08	653.10	637.11	15.99
30-May-08	639.15	628.79	10.36
6-Jun-08	639.15	618.99	20.16
13-Jun-08	618.86	607.34	11.52
20-Jun-08	608.81	597.13	11.68
27-Jun-08	583.95	575.37	8.58
4-Jul-08	582.75	566.81	15.94
11-Aug-08	580.57	555.99	24.58
18-Sep-08	593.02	579.09	13.93

	13Wk2Sig=	9.75
	4Wk2Sig=	13.30

The volatility for OEX in 2008 year has been extreme, so both the 6 month an the 3 month 2 sigma (standard deviation) has been computed for OEX, along with the usual 13 month 2 sig. Please note that the 13 month computation is less than the 6 month or 13 month computations, because of the 2008 volatility.

Each underlying stock and indices has a similar computation of the 6 month 2 sigma for the sheet of the underlying in SelfAdapDTN4.

So as you may see the worksheet for OEX which is similar to that for the SPX and the other 19 underlying stocks is very helpful in both the WWI triggered Long position trading as well as the OEX CCSS monthly income generation trading. The TradeForm already described above also computes 2 sigma Short Call and Short Put for to be used for the OEX CCSS, and for the stocks CCSS such as for AAPL, RIMM, RIO, SPY, & QQQQ. During 2005 when GOOG had a fantastic rise in price, I found that using 2 sigma Put GOOG CCSS were profitable. Using Puts was safer than using Calls because of the increase which often exceeded a 2 sigma rise which would have endangered the short Call of a GOOG CCSS.

I will use GOOG as an example of the stock worksheets. On 15 Dec 05 WWI triggered a Long Put for GOOG since WWI = 81.28, the next day the Long P430 was executed. The next day (19th Dec) the WWI dropped to 63.41, therefore the Long Put 430 was closed to make a one day profit of $300 for a cost of $8,690. The return = 3.5% for the one day trade. This example shows why WWI 0triggered Longs are a good way to increment the Monthly profit of CCSS trades.

Figure 6.4 shows a portion of the Command Center **worksheet** as a the Indices and some of the stocks tracked by SelfAdapDTN4.xls. The command center sheet also tracks all of the options and special items such as weekly OEX options, QLD & QID and the OEX Spread options for the current month.

Figure 6.4

SelfAdapStkOp4.xls Comand Center

12-Sep-08 Open Sep Spreads   Current Brker Capital $25,000

Name	Symbol	Last	Del	Bid	Ask	Low	Hi	Vol
S&P 100 INDEX	OEX.XO	577.64	-1.24	0.00	0.00	570.63	579.89	0.00
S&P 500 INDEX	SPX.XO	1,250.47	1.42	0.00	0.00	1233.81	1255.09	0.00
DOW JONES 30 INDUSTRIALS	INDU.X	11,421.26	-12.45	0.00	0.00	11280.40	11459.93	88943029.00
NASDAQ COMPOSITE INDEX (COMBINED)	COMPX.X	2,260.37	2.15	0.00	0.00	2228.00	2268.83	0.00
CBOE VOLATILITY INDEX (S&P 500)	VIX.XO	25.39	1.00	0.00	0.00	24.80	25.52	0.00
AMGEN INC	AMGN	62.94	-0.45	62.94	62.95	62.42	63.45	3236408.00
CISCO SYSTEMS INC	CSCO	23.15	0.10	23.14	23.15	22.61	23.30	20348802.00
DELL INC	DELL	19.25	0.07	19.24	19.25	18.82	19.26	10687768.00
GENENTECH INC	DNA	96.63	-0.47	96.64	96.65	96.05	97.26	1473078.00
EBAY INC	EBAY	22.67	-0.36	22.67	22.68	22.39	22.92	5692272.00
GOOGLE INC A	GOOG	439.80	6.05	439.75	439.97	429.00	441.99	3500409.00
ISHARES TR RUSSELL 2000	IWM	72.03	0.11	72.02	72.03	71.04	72.39	51966113.00
INTERNATIONAL BUSINESS MACHINE	IBM	118.64	-0.56	118.61	118.64	116.82	119.00	2746088.00
INTEL CORP	INTC	19.96	-0.23	19.95	19.96	19.58	20.13	26448895.00
NETFLIX INC	NFLX	29.59	0.76	29.55	29.58	28.32	29.70	469104.00
MICROSOFT CORP	MSFT	27.54	0.20	27.53	27.54	26.94	27.62	31090773.00
NETFLIX INC	NFLX	29.59	0.76	29.55	29.58	28.32	29.70	469104.00
ORACLE CORP	ORCL	19.26	-0.09	19.26	19.27	19.04	19.49	14746812.00
OCCIDENTAL PETROLEUM CP	OXY	72.50	2.64	72.49	72.51	70.02	72.80	3362856.00
POWERSHRS QQQ TR SR1 ETF	QQQQ	43.49	-0.11	43.48	43.49	42.90	43.71	94094869.00
SINA CORPORATION	SINA	39.43	1.35	39.42	39.46	37.09	39.74	802714.00
SIRIUS XM RADIO INC	SIRI	0.89	-0.03	0.89	0.89	0.87	0.91	21403417.00
SPDR TRUST SR 1 ETF	SPY	125.61	0.10	125.61	125.62	123.83	125.98	122679513.00

CBOE DELAYED QUOTES FOR OEX

The workbook SelfAdapDTN4.xls has sheets for entering by copying from the CBOE website and pasting in special sheets set up for that purpose to the left of the OEX sheet. A sample sheet for the OEX quotes called CBOECmdCntr is shown in Figure 6.5 below:

Figure 6.5

CBOE QUOTES

OEX (S&P 100 INDEX)   675.95 -9.70
Jan 02, 2008 @ 16:55 ET

Calls	Last Sal	Net	Bid	Ask	Vol	Open Int Puts	Last Sal	Net	Bid
08 Jan 680.00 (RZA AP-E)	3.5	-.4	3.7	4.2	502	0 08 Jan 680.00 (RZA MP-E)	6.3	2.4	5.7
08 Jan 685.00 (RZA AQ-E)	1.7	-5.5	1.75	1.95	201	13 08 Jan 685.00 (RZA MQ-E)	11	6.1	8.6
08 Jan 690.00 (RZA AR-E)	0.6	-4.7	0.6	0.85	555	45 08 Jan 690.00 (RZA MR-E)	14	7	13.3
08 Jan 695.00 (RZA AS-E)	0.25	-1.55	0.15	0.3	149	101 08 Jan 695.00 (RZA MS-E)	9	0	18.2
08 Jan 700.00 (RZA AT-E)	0.15	-.07	0.05	0.25	75	59 08 Jan 700.00 (RZA MT-E)	11.4	0	23
08 Jan 705.00 (RZA AA-E)	0.05	-.055	0	0.2	33	25 08 Jan 705.00 (RZA MA-E)	0	0	28
08 Jan 710.00 (RZA AB-E)	0.05	-.01	0.05	0.1	250	73 08 Jan 710.00 (RZA MB-E)	0	0	33
08 Jan 500.00 (OEB AT-E)	188.9	0	179.2	180.2	0	1 08 Jan 500.00 (OEB MT-E)	0.05	0	0
08 Jan 520.00 (OEB AD-E)	0	0	159.2	160.2	0	0 08 Jan 520.00 (OEB MD-E)	0.05	0	0
08 Jan 535.00 (OEB AG-E)	0	0	144.2	145.2	0	0 08 Jan 535.00 (OEB MG-E)	0.05	0	0
08 Jan 540.00 (OEB AH-E)	154.5	0	139.2	140.2	0	15 08 Jan 540.00 (OEB MH-E)	0.05	0	0
08 Jan 545.00 (OEB AI-E)	0	0	134.3	135.3	0	0 08 Jan 545.00 (OEB MI-E)	0.15	0	0
08 Jan 550.00 (OEB AJ-E)	0	0	129.3	130.3	0	0 08 Jan 550.00 (OEB MJ-E)	0.2	0	0
08 Jan 555.00 (OEB AK-E)	0	0	124.3	125.3	0	0 08 Jan 555.00 (OEB MK-E)	0.1	0	0
08 Jan 560.00 (OEB AL-E)	126.1	0	119.3	120.3	0	10 08 Jan 560.00 (OEB ML-E)	0.1	0	0
08 Jan 565.00 (OEB AM-E)	0	0	114.3	115.3	0	0 08 Jan 565.00 (OEB MM-E)	0.1	0	0

The CBOE quotes are obtained from website: http://www.cboe.com/ To obtain the above data, go to the website, click on OEX, and then when the OEX screen appears, click on ALL to get the weekly quotes and all other Call & Put option quotes, which are 15 minutes delayed.

The CBOE quote for OEX is shown above in Figure 6.5. The first 11 rows of the quote show the newly introduced weekly quotes that were first introduced 28 Oct 2005. These weekly expiring options are introduced each Monday (or the first trading day of the Week) and expire each Friday of the option trading month. These weekly options permit you to take advantage of special events such as large stock market movements caused by economic reports. I took advantage of using OEX Put CCSS using Short P580=RZD XP and Long P575=RZD XO on Monday of Christmas week with expiration on Friday of Christmas week because traditionally the OEX rises during Christmas week. When the weekly P580/575 was opened on Monday the initial credit was 1.8. At expiration on Friday the OEX was 579.41 which made the P580/575 = 580-579.41 = 0.59. So the profit for the 5 days was = 1.8 − 0.59 = 1.21 or for 10 options the Profit = 10*100*1.21 − Commission =1210-74 = $1,136. The Margin for the 10 weekly options = 5*100*2 = $10,000. So the return on margin = 1136*10000 = 11.4% for the 5 day trade. Please notice, I am not recommending such trades, but this example shows how the Weeklys can be used for 5 day CCSS. At this time the range of strike prices is not wide enough to select 2 sigma CCSS, so this strategy is too risky for Weeklys. However, a strategy that seems to work better is to use the closer in spreads but don't open until Thu or Fri for the Weeklys that expire at close on Friday.

TRADING USING OEX WEEKLYS

I believe the Weeklys, introduced 28th Oct 2005, offer a new opportunity for making profits using 2 sigma Covered Credit Short Spreads. After only 8 weeks (on Christmas 2005) the volume of trading and the breadth of strike prices is increasing making it more practical to open 2sig CCSS positions. Two sheets have been added to SelfAdapStkOp to aid in computing safe Weekly CCSS positions:

Weeklys to the right of OEX sheet which computes the one week 2 sigmas as well as OEX & SPX CCSS positions. The OEX strike prices are 5 apart and the SPX strike prices are 15 points apart. The most favorable Weekly CCSS positions shown. Figure 6.6 is a portion of the SelfAdapDTN4 Trading Center Sheet showing the weekly spreads for expiration of the day for:

12 Sep 08: Fig 6.6

P555/565 Wkly	1.35	0.27	$653	$1,054	$5,000	33.12%
C580/585 Wkly	1.35	0.80	$1,328	$526	$1,656	$851

In general, Weeklys have the same contract specifications as standard options, except for the time to expiration. New series are listed each Friday, expiring the following Friday. (The exception being that no Weeklys will be listed that expire the third Friday of the month – the expiration week for standard options).

- This is an example of opening 5 OEX weekly C580/585 and 2 P555/565 that yields an Initial Credit = $906 for a Margin = $2500. As may be seen this condor yields a high return on Margin = 36.24%. The question is: How safe is this Weekly Condor? When the market is very volatile, the limited number of strike prices for Weeklys make it difficult to find a safe condor. My Rule: wait until near market close on Thu or near open Fri to open the credit spreads to reduce risk. By then you may see how the weekly condors will fare.

Both SPX and OEX Weeklys are cash-settled contracts and offer the same continuous, two-sided quotes as standard options. SPX Weeklys are European-style exercise with A.M. settlement, and OEX Weeklys are American-style exercise with P.M. settlement. I only use OEX weeklys with the RZA symbols.

THE GREEKS – Statistical percentages

These sensitivities of the Option price to the underlying market value are expressed in 5 Greek alphabet symbols: delta, gamma, theta, vega and rho   which will be explained below:

- Delta: Change in Option price per change in Underlying market; for example if the OEX Call 590 = 6.5 & Call 595 = 3.8, then delta = (6.5-3.8)/(595-590) = 0.54, which is the slope of the option price to OEX change. In other words if the OEX rose by 1 point, the Call 590 would rise by 0.54 points. How to use? If the C590 = 6.5, and the OEX rose by 1, then the C590 would rise to 6.5+0.54 = 7.04
- Gamma: Sensitivity of Delta to change in the Underlying. Gamma represents a change in Delta. For example if Gamma change or 0.2, then the Delta in the previous example = Delta + Gamma = 0.54 +0.2 = 0.74

- Theta: Sensitivity of options value to change in time. For example it you opened a 2 sigma Call Covered Credit Spread short Call 605 & long Call 605 and your received 1.1 points for the spread, then at options expiration 25 trading days later, the spread expires worthless, then the Call Spread Theta = 1.1/25 = 0.044 points/day.

- Vega: Sensitivity of options value to change in volatility. Vega is an absolute change in options value for a percentage change in volatility. For example on a day when the OEX = 590.26 at close the C590 = 6.0, the Volatility = 11.57 a increase of 0.62 = 0.62/11.57 = 5.36 %. Then the C590 = 6.0 + .05 = 6.05 due to Vega or the volatility factor.

- Rho: Sensitivity of options value to change in interest rate. Rho is the absolute change in options value for 1 % change in interest rate. For example on the Day the Fed raised the interest rate by 0.25%, the OEX Call 590 = 7.80, and the C590 dropped to 7.20 or a drop of 0.6 immediately after the Fed announced the rise, then *Rho = 0.6/0.25 = 2.4* in this example.

Part 2 Spread Sheet Tools for Index Options Trading

Chapter 7 WWI Charts for Currency Trading

This book was originally written when I lived in Spain before I met my Currency Trading expert, Francisco from Madrid. We conducted a short course on Options and Currency trading and we jointly discovered that the Welles-Wilder Indicator, a signal I used for deciding when to Buy Calls and Puts would also work as a trigger for Buying and Selling Lots of Currencies. The trigger works as in the Currency Command Center sheet taken from my SelfAdapCur software shown **Figure 7.1 below**:

An Introduction to Currency Vocabulary:

1.   **Lot**: refers to an amount of currency which is usually $100,000 or the forex or foreign currency exchange.

2.   **Pips**: are the smallest part of a Lot which varies for the different currencies. Currency trading doesn't pay commissions, the brokers obtain the number of Pips between Bid and Ask which varies for the different currencies as follows in the **Figure 7.1 below**

Figure 7.1

CURRENCY TRADING COMMAND CENTER

					Buy	Sell
$/Euro = 1.2644		0.7909	Euro/$	# Lots= 1		
SelfAdaptiveStkOp		MF Prft =		Put	Comm=	
Date	Underlying	Bid	Ask	Del	WWI	
12-Sep-08	Euro/$	1.4075	1.4078	-1.4075	61.75	Buy
12-Sep-08	YEN/$	107.1100	107.1105	-107.1100	41.14	Sell
12-Sep-08	$/GBP	1.7678	1.81	-1.7678	43.11	Sell
12-Sep-08	$/CHF	1.1367	1.1372	-1.1367	70.60	Buy
12-Sep-08	eur-yenHdge	1.0573	1.0975		55.17	

WWI Triggers	*WWI<20*	*WWI>80*	Ask - Bid	*Pip Size*		Bu
Euro/$	*Sell*	*Buy*	3 pips	0.0001	Position	
YEN/$	*Buy*	*Sell*	5 pips	0.0001	Bot $/Eur	
$/GBP	*Sell*	*Buy*	4 pips	0.01	Sell $/Eur	
$/CHF	*Sell*	*Buy*	5 pips	0.0001	Buy$/Eur	

	Sld	Del	Prft	105.7025	
YEN/$	0.0278	114.0722	$99,602		Sell$/Eur
12-Sep-08	9:58:26				

Rate	Last	Ystd Close	% Chng	2006 Open	YTD	MTD
EURUSD	1.4075	1.3947	0.92%	1.1832	18.96%	-4.04%
USDJPY	107.11	106.7	0.38%	118	-9.23%	-1.54%
GBPUSD	1.7678	1.7522	0.89%	1.72	2.78%	-2.95%
USDCHF	1.1367	1.1391	-0.21%	1.3146	-13.53%	3.22%

3.   **RollOver**: refers to the overnight charge on open currency positions which is usually the number of pips in the Ask-Bid column in Figure 7.1 above.

When the position is short (Sold the Lot) you receive a listed credit in your account for each Lot or fraction of a Lot. I like to use 0.2 Lots. When you are Long (Bought the Lot) you receive a listed debit in your account for each Lot or fraction of a Lot.

4.   **$/Del**: refers to the sensitivity in Dollars of the currency in the smallest part (pip) of the currency In the **Figure** Also in the upper right hand corner of the figure are the ratios between $ and other currencies expanded in Fig 7.2 below:

$/CHF	$78,838
YEN/$	$873
$/GDB	$100,000

7.3 below are shown some typical trades of USD relative to Eur, Yen, SF (Swiss Franc) and UK pound.

Figure 7.3
Settled Trades

						TotRlOvr	-$33.00		$/CHF	$78,838	
						Cap Now=	$3,613		YEN/$	$873	
									$/GDB	$100,000	

Ticket#(S#) acc.currency	Currency ConvRate	Buy/Sell	Units	Open	Close	Currency P/L	ConvRate	Comm	RollOver	P/L
2417379 (0)	USDJPY	Buy	1	120.91	120.81	-10000.00 JPY	120.81	0	$0.00	-$82.77
2417382 (0)	USDJPY	Buy	1	120.95	120.81	-14000.00 JPY	120.81	0	$0.00	-$115.88
2419026 (0)	USDJPY	Sell	1	120.84	120.88	-4000.00 JPY	120.84	0	$0.00	-$33.10
2419054 (0)	USDCAD	Buy	2	1.1589	1.1577	-240.00 CAD	1.1577	0	$0.00	-$207.31
2419064 (0)	USDJPY	Buy	1	120.88	121.01	13000.00 JPY	121.05	0	$0.00	$107.39
2421201 (0)	GBPUSD	Sell	1	1.7527	1.7529	-20.00 USD	1	0	$0.00	-$20.00
2422718 (0)	GBPUSD	Sell	1	1.7518	1.7558	-400.00 USD	1	0	$0.00	-$400.00
2422897 (0)	GBPUSD	Sell	1	1.755	1.753	200.00 USD	1	0	-$12.50	$187.50

For example if 1 Lot of $/Euro changes by 0.0020 or 20 pips, then the value of the position would change by .0020*100,000 = $200; if 1 lot of $/CHF changes by 0.0020 or 20 pips, then the value of the position would change by .0020*78,838 = $157.68; if one lot of Yen/$ changes by .2 or 20 pips, then the value of the position would change by .2*873 = $174.6; if 1 Lot of $/GBP changes by .0020 or 20 pips, then the value of the position would change by .0020*100,00 = $200.

The parameters to use for computing the cost, and profit or loss of a trade is given below in the Computation Summary Section of the Currency Command Center (CurCmdCntr) sheet of my currency trading software package. The equations for the computations contained in Figure 7.5 below are as follows:

- *Cost* if the trade is a **Buy** or *Credit* if the trade is a **Sell = #Lots*$/Del*CurrVal**
- *Profit (or Loss) = $/Del*TrdDel*

I believe it is important to create such spread sheets to aid you in your currency trading.

Figure 7.4 is given below that shows how to compute the Trade Cost and Profit on the Euro covered by my SelfAdapCur.xls software package.

Figure 7.4

12-Sep-08 **EUR**	$0 Sell	1.4075	-0.0050 Del
use Ctrl"x" to enter data from yhoo		Prft =	$100
EUR	$100 Buy	1.4025	

I have now given you a brief introduction to Currency Trading. I believe you need to do the following things to be a successful currency trader:

1.   Create your own trading Spread sheets or obtain my Currency Trading Software: SelfAdapCur.xls (cost $70).

2.   Learn how to use your currency trading software by opening a free Demo Account. I investigated several before selecting Mgforex who had easy to download software for their trading platform at:

http://www.mgforex.com/ENG/basics/content/welcome.asp?u=D-169971

3.   I find that it is easy to make mistakes in currency trading, so the 30 day training period allowed by the free Demo Account is necessary to avoid errors during Live Trading that could cost you several hundred dollars in just a few minutes. *I must warn you: Currency Trading is a risky business and you could lose more capital than you have in your currency account!*

4.   Adapt a trading System. I find using the Welles-Wilder Indicator shown in Table 7.1 above gives good results. It does not always result in profit, but I believe by paying close daily attention to the currency markets. I obtain real time currency data from MGforex which I can copy and paste into the Currency Control Center of my SelfAdapCur software using a Macro actuated by CntrlX, or a similar spread sheet you may desire to create. I believe it would be difficult to profit from currency trading without a reliable trading system. I have also developed a trigger based on the prediction made by a 20 day moving average of the currency to be useful.

I should emphasize that currency trading gives 100:1 leverage on your trading capital. The margin for one Lot is $1,000. For example as may be seen in Figure 7.4 above, 1 Lot of Euro costs $119,000 and the currency broker would require a margin of $1000; 1.5 Lots of CHF (Swiss Franc) cost $155,000 and the currency broker would require a margin of $1500; 2 Lots of Yen could cost $211,000 and the broker would require $2000 margin; 0.8 Lot of British Pounds would cost 141,760 and the margin would be $800. Note: I also use 0.2 or a Lot for active trading.

Remember leverage lets you trade and earn large returns on limited capital in a short time, but it also represents a high risk should the market move precipitously against your open currency position. Since currency moves can be caused by world events such as terrorist attacks or World Bank announcements, it is good to close-out open currency positions as soon as possible and before

the week-end. ***Don't be greedy: take $200 on a 1 Lot which is a 20% return on Margin. This can often be done in a single day!***
        The Control Center of the CurCmdCntr sheet of was shown in Fig 7.1 above.

        A Macro is invoked by clicking CntrlX after copying the real time quotes from MGforex which then pastes the quotes in the correct sections of the CurCmdCntr sheet in Figure 7.1 above.

Jon Schiller's Currency Trading Strategy

        When a Currency shows a WWI trigger of > 80 or <20 , then execute a position as indicated by Table 7.1 above.
        1.   On the Mgforex trading platform to open a position click on the currency quote and a Pop-up will show the selected currency Sell 1 Lot *at Market*; your must select Buy if you want. I always open the position *at Market* .
        2.   After the position is opened and confirmed by the Trade Account Status sheet of the Mgforex website. On the trading platform, go to the selected currency, click and place a close order at *Limit* and enter a limit price that would give a profit of $200 to $300.
        Usually the intraday currency volatility is enough to give a close within the trading day which ends at 3PM NY time or 12 Noon Los Angeles time.
        If you use the WWI trigger for opening positions, you can expect about one trigger per week. I have prepared a profit projection based on this strategy, and if you have no losses and when your trading capital increases by $5,000 increase the # Lots by one. For example if you should open a trading account with $2,500 and start trading with 1 Lot, I recommend waiting until you reach $10,000 in your account before increasing the # Lots to 2; at $15,000 capital increase the # Lots to 3, and so forth.
        Figure 7.5 shows the capital growth of such a strategy *without losses.* Figure 7.8 shows the capital growth of this strategy with one loss per month of about the same size as the profits of the successful months. ***Please note these Figures are not***

a Promise, but are merely mathematical projections (performed with Excel) what could be achieved if the stated assumptions are met.

Figure 7.5 One Year Projections of Currency Trading Capital Growth

CAPITAL GROWTH USING Forex WW Triggered Currencies   When Capital Grows from $2,500 to $10,000 switch from 1 Lot to 2 Lots

Beginning Capital = $2,500 $8,422 after 6 Mo
C+P pm   1.1 SSCom=   7.16666 $20,260 after 1 Year

WeekEnd	Currency	Buy/Sell	Units	Del	$/Del	Profit	Capital	RollOver	P/L w/RlOvr	%Ret/Mgn	SumNetPrft
20-Jan-06	Yen	1	114.34	0.34	$873	$297	$2,785	-$12	$285	10.23%	$285
27-Jan-06	Euro	1		0.003	$100,000	$300	$3,085	$0	$300	9.72%	$585
3-Feb-06	C+F	1		0.008	$78,838	$300	$3,384	$0	$300	8.85%	$884
10-Feb-06	GDB	1		0.003	$100,000	$300	$3,684	$0	$300	8.14%	$1,184
17-Feb-06	Yen	1	114.34	0.34	$873	$297	$3,969	-$12	$285	7.18%	$1,469
24-Feb-06	Euro	1		0.003	$100,000	$300	$4,269	$0	$300	7.03%	$1,769
3-Mar-06	C+F	1		0.008	$78,838	$300	$4,569	$0	$300	6.58%	$2,069
10-Mar-06	GDB	1		0.003	$100,000	$300	$4,869	$0	$300	6.16%	$2,369
17-Mar-06	Yen	1	114.34	0.34	$873	$297	$5,154	-$12	$285	5.53%	$2,654
23-Mar-06	Euro	1		0.003	$100,000	$300	$5,454	$0	$300	5.50%	$2,954
31-Mar-06	C+F	1		0.008	$78,838	$300	$5,753	$0	$300	5.21%	$3,253
7-Apr-06	GDB	1		0.003	$100,000	$300	$6,053	$0	$300	4.98%	$3,553

I left out the date from April to Dec 06 to shorten the figure, which continues below.

29-Dec-06	Euro	2		0.003	$100,000	$300	$19,079	$0	$300	1.57%	$16,579
5-Jan-07	C+F	2		0.008	$78,838	$300	$19,378	$0	$300	1.55%	$16,878
12-Jan-07	GDB	2		0.003	$100,000	$300	$19,678	$0	$300	1.52%	$17,178
19-Jan-07	Yen	2	114.34	0.34	$873	$594	$20,260	-$12	$582	2.87%	$17,760
26-Jan-07	Euro	2		0.003	$100,000	$300	$20,560	$0	$300	1.46%	$18,060
2-Feb-07	C+F	2		0.008	$78,838	$300	$20,860	$0	$300	1.44%	$18,360
9-Feb-07	GDB	2		0.003	$100,000	$300	$21,160	$0	$300	1.42%	$18,660

As may be noted from the figure the initial capital of $2500 increases to $18,660 if the trading assumptions are met.

I performed the same projections in a different Excel worksheet, but this time I assumed one monthly loss about the same as the weekly profits for the successful months. The end of the time period results are shown in the Excel 9 Feb 07 line below, which can be **compared with the last line of Figure 7.8, immediately below**:

With this level of losses, which is a reasonable worst case assumption, the Currency Trading Capital had grown to $11,215 instead of the no loss case of $18,660, still a 4.5 times or 450% gain in one year. This figure shows that good Trading Capital Growth can be achieved even with one loss per month or some 12 losses during the trading year.

Mgforex has an excellent electronic trading platform:

http://www.mgforex.com/ENG/basics/content/welcome.asp?u=D-169971

You can register for a Demo (demonstration) account to learn how to use the trading platform before risking capital in currency trading. One lot of currencies is about $100,000. You may also use sublots. I like to use 0.2 sublot = 0.2*100,000 =$20,000. Currently my SelfAdapCur program uses 0.2 lots.

MGforex has a nice feature at their website allowing you to check with trades made and completed. Here are some examples using the Demo account while learning how to use their electronic platform in the tables below:

Figure 7.6 are some example demo *Settled Trades*

Settled Trades									
Ticket#(SM)	Currency	Buy/Sell	Units	Open	Close	Currency P/L	ConvRate	Comm	Rollover
acccurrency	ConvRate								
2417379 (0)	USDJPY	Buy	1	120.91	120.81	-10000.00 JPY	120.81	0	.00 USD
2417382 (0)	USDJPY	Buy	1	120.95	120.81	-14000.00 JPY	120.81	0	.00 USD
2419026 (0)	USDJPY	Sell	1	120.84	120.88	-4000.00 JPY	120.84	0	.00 USD
2419054 (0)	USDCAD	Buy	2	1.1589	1.1577	-240.00 CAD	1.1577	0	.00 USD
2419064 (0)	USDJPY	Buy	1	120.88	121.01	13000.00 JPY	121.05	0	.00 USD
2421201 (0)	GBPUSD	Sell	1	1.7527	1.7529	-20.00 USD	1	0	.00 USD
2422718 (0)	GBPUSD	Sell	1	1.7518	1.7558	-400.00 USD	1	0	.00 USD
2422897 (0)	GBPUSD	Sell	1	1.755	1.753	200.00 USD	1	0	-12.50 USD

Table 7.7 on the next page is an Example of demo ***Open Orders and Open Trades*** before they are ***Settled Trades***

It is easy to make errors, so you should be careful in making the orders.

Table 7.7

31-Jan-06								
Open Orders								
Order#(SY)	Currency	Buy/Sell	Units	Type	Stop	Limit	Time	Date
5504608 (O)	USD.JPY	Sell	1	Limit	0	117.5	14:53:53	1/31/2006
							Prft If Ex	
		Yen	1	117.3	0.2	$873	$175	
Open Trades								
Ticket#(SY)	Currency	Buy/Sell	Units	Amount	Open	Close	ConvRate	Comm
2484309 (O)	EUR.USD	Buy	2	0.2	1.2228	1.2142	1	.00 USD
2488128 (O)	USD.JPY	Buy	1	0.1	117.3	117.34	117.38	.00 USD

Part 2 Spread Sheet Tools for Index Options Trading

Chapter 8 Decision Charts Generated from SelfAdapSigIndicOEX

This chapter gets down to the brass tacks of how you generate a chart from your Excel spread sheets. The Signal Indicator workbook is SelfAdapSigIndicOEX.xls which is used to generate the decision charts most helpful in your OEX option trading. You will see how to select the right columns from your spread sheet to be the series (the data) in your chart; how to select the type of chart you want (e.g. line chart, bar chart, combination chart, 3D chart, etc.); how to edit the title, axis name, and how to label the points on your curves or bar charts to show the quantity. It's all easy with Microsoft's Excel spread sheet program. I will also show you how to take an existing chart used for the current month, and then edit it to use for the next option month. The charts discussed in this section are the ones I use regularly to help me with my option trading strategies. This workbook, SelfAdapSigIndicOEX is available from the author to be downloaded as an email attachment as described in Appendix A. One very useful sheet in this workbook is shown in Figure 8.1 below which is a 3 level Neural Network using data from the various signal indicators to determine the OEX market trend Up, Down or trendless at the end of each trading day.

Please Note: The charts in this chapter are not intended to be read, but to show the format the charts appear when you acquire my software.

Figure 8.1

Figure 8.1	Feed Forward Neural Network				Output>10 Uptrend			Output>-10&<10 Directionless		
	5 Input, 3 Layer, 1 Output				Output<-10 Downtrend					
	OEX =	573.23	del = -5.65		12-Sep-08	10:39:32	OUTPUT			
Mkt Sig	Input	Wtg2	Layer 1	3	Layer 2	Wtg3	Layer 3	Dntrnd	Uptrnd	
Mad4	-1.94	0.632911	-1.229695	0.333333	-0.41	10	-37.64	-1	0	Layer 3
Mad9-4	-4.91	0.387597	-1.902237	0.333333	-0.63			-1	0	Strong
MADC	-2.06		2.5	-5.155263	0.333333	-1.72			-1	0	Very Strong
Sto%K-%D	-282.50	0.010635	-3.00436	0.333333	-1.00			0	0	Subject to Rapid Reversal
WWI	41.63	0								
		0								
Total =	-291.41		-11.29		-3.76					
Mad200	578.82									
MxOpMo	599.84	Delta	2*2sig	Volatility						
MnOpMo	568.98	30.86	80.03	38.56%						

Note that Layer 3 in the OUTPUT at this trading day shows a down trend, subject to a Rapid Reversal in the Up direction. If the Layer 3 output is greater than 10 it indicates an Up Trend (Uptrnd) as 1: if Layer 3 output is less than -10 it indicates a Down Trend (Dntrnd) as -1. Since Layer 3 is -54.48 the market is *5 layers on down trend, subject to rapid up movement.*

CHART MAD4

Figure 8.2 below shows the OEX MADC, which is a popular signal indicator. Chart generated from SelfAdapSigIndicOEX.xls workbook. This same workbook generates these other charts as well: MAD9-4, MADC, Stochastics %K-%D, CumDel, Bollinger Band, OverBot-OverSld, Stochastics and WWI, MADC & WWI, MAD9-4 & WWI, MAD4 & WWI, SAMN Candlestick, 10 Day RVI – RSI & OEX. So as you may see this Workbook is a rich source of Signal Indicator Charts and their algorithms. Since several of these charts were presented in Chapter 1, 3, and 4, they will not be repeated here. Mad4 plotted versus OEX is a valuable chart and is simple to generate shown below.

Fig 8.2 OEX MADC

MADC & OEX

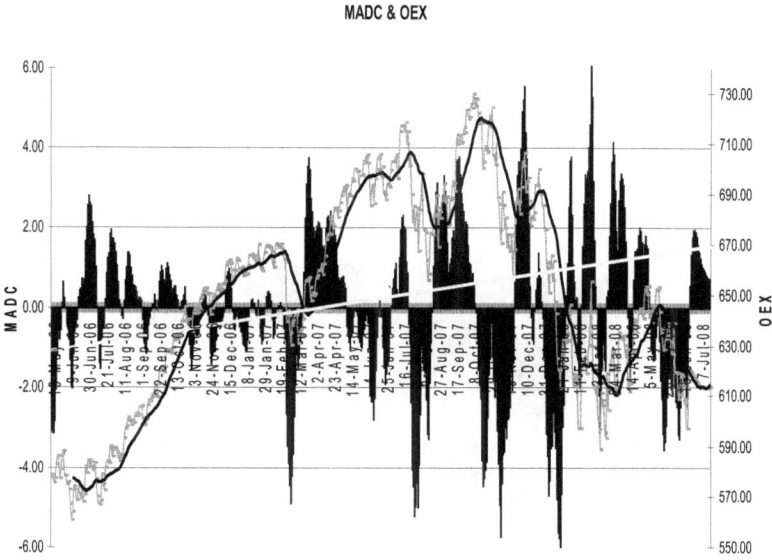

The MADC black bars are positive during an **up** movement; down bars show a **down** movement.

Figure 8.3 below show the CumDel (cumulative difference) over a two year period. You may see we have had a bull increase until Oct 07 then a bear plunge until Feb 08, a recovery in Apr – May 08 then another pull back to near the Feb 08 lows. You may see the charts are helpful in making trading decisions.

Dr. Jon Schiller

Figure 8.3 CumDel

CumDelta & OEX

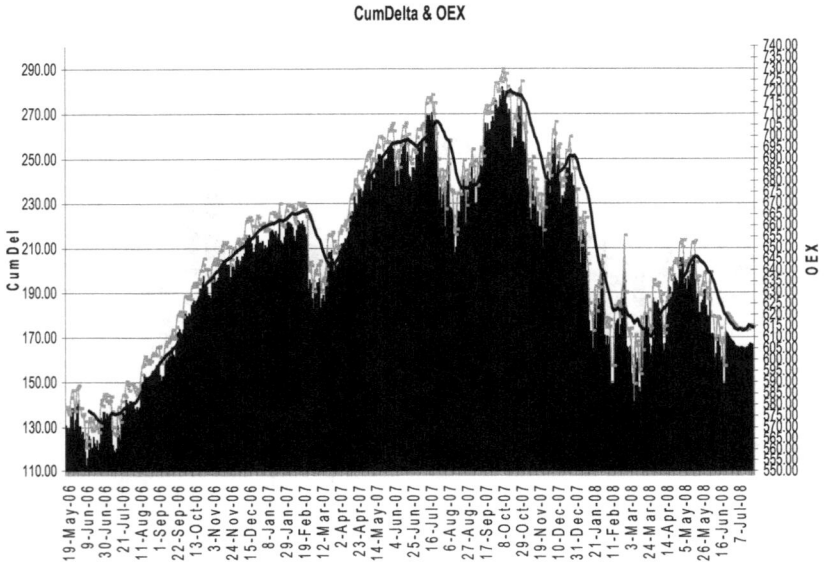

Figure 8.4 shows the Bollinger-Band which is a pictorial way of showing when the OEX is overbought (above the UpBand) and oversold (below the LoBand). Note when the OEX is overbought, this is a signal that a down movement is coming; when oversold, this is a signal for a coming rise in the OEX.

Figure 8.4 OEX Bollinger-Band

OEX black & Bollinger Bands Grn UpBand, Red LoBand

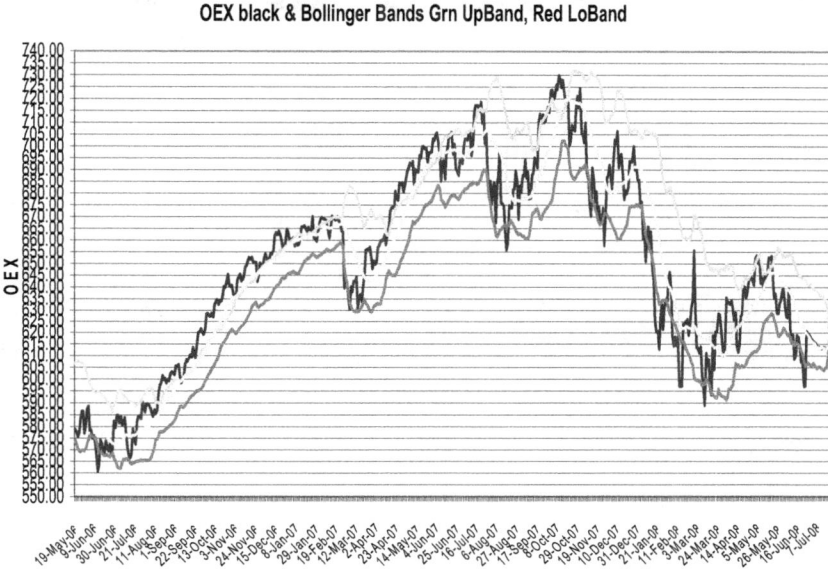

Figure 8.5 below shows the correlation between the WWI & Bollinger Band indicators for the OEX being Oversold & Overbought. The Bollinger black & WWI green for Oversold signaling a rise coming; Bollinger red & WWI yellow for Overbought signaling a drop is coming.

Figure 8.5 OEX WWI & Bollinger-Band Correlation

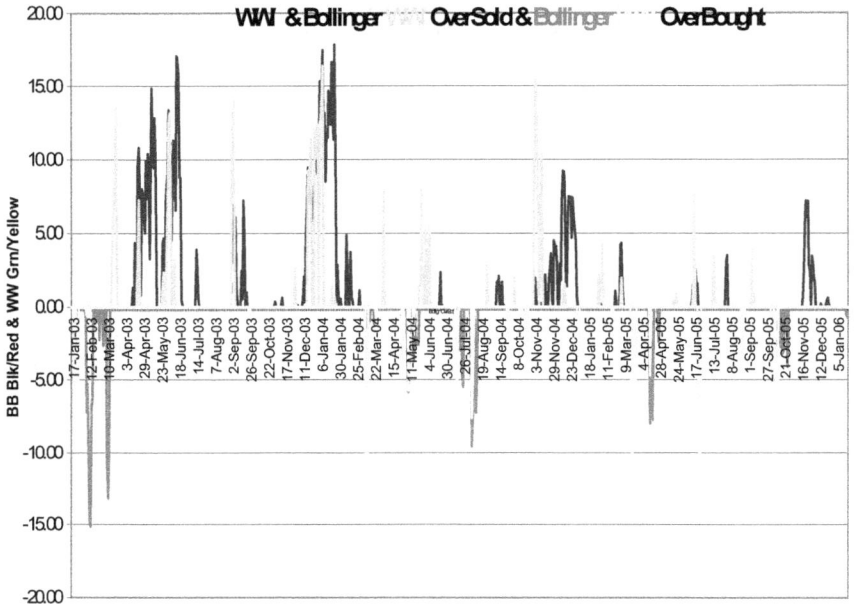

Figure 8.6 below shows the correlation between Stochastics %K-%D and WWI The Stochastics %K-%D are shown as black bars and the WWI is shown as a red curve with 50 day moving average trend line for WWI shown as a black curve. Both the Stochastics and the WWI are good indicators. However, it is easier to create logical triggers for buying Calls & Puts with the WWI than the stochastics since the WWI logic triggers are: Buy Calls for WWI<20; buy Puts for WWI>80.

Figure 8.6 OEX Stochastics %K-%D & WWI Correlation

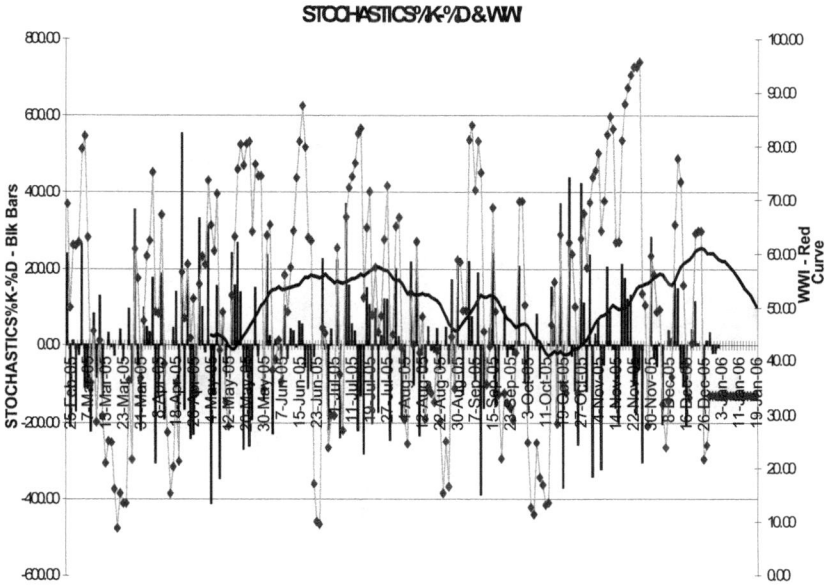

STOCHASTICS%K-%D&WWI

Figure 8.7 below shows the correlation between the MADC & WWI signal indicators. The MADC are shown as black bars and the OEX WWI are shown as the Red Curve. Note that when the MADC is positive the WWI is above 50 and when MADC is negative the WW is less than 50 – this is the main correlation between these two signal indicators.

Dr. Jon Schiller

Figure 8.7 OEX MADC & WWI Correlation

MADC&WWI

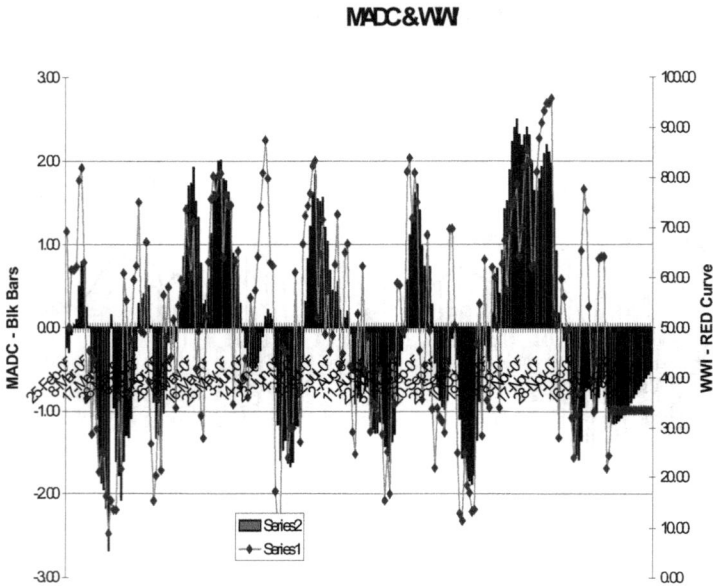

Figure 8.8 shows the correlation between MAD9-4 & WWI signal indicators. You may see the close correlation between these two signal indicators, with the correlation between plus and minus MAD9-4 and the 50 level for the WWI. When the WWI is greater than 80 a drop is coming. When the MAD9-4 is above 5 this is a signal for a coming drop in the OEX. When the WWI < 20 this is a signal for a coming rise. When the MADC9-4 is less than -5 this signals a coming rise.

Figure 8.8 OEX MAD9-4 & WWI Correlation

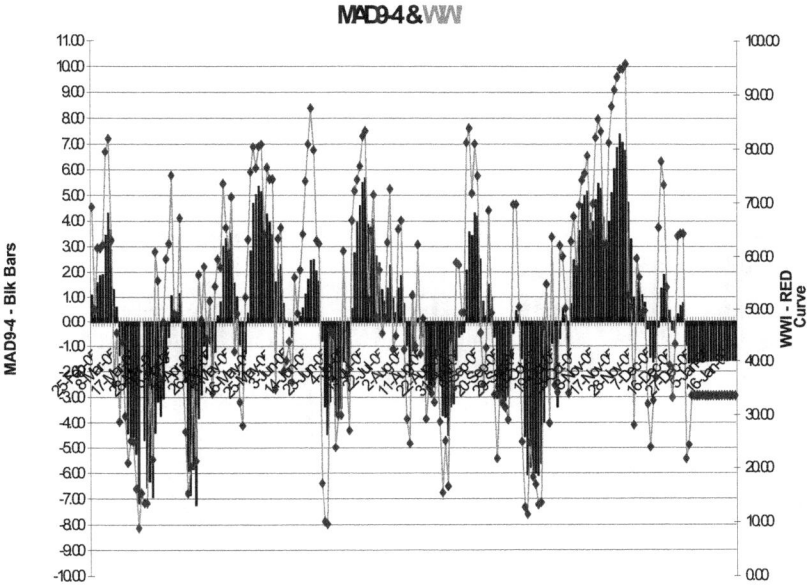

Figure 8.9 portrays the correlation between the MAD4 and WWI signal indicators. When MAD4 is less than -4 and when WWI < 20 this signals a rise is coming. When the MAD4 > 3 and WWI > 80, that is a signal for over bought conditions and a drop is on the horizon.

Dr. Jon Schiller

Figure 8.9 OEX MAD4 & WWI Correlation

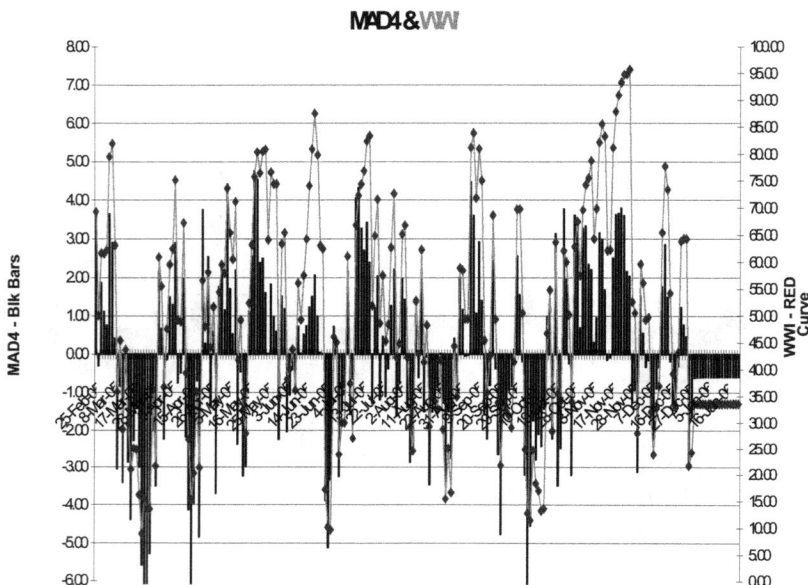

MAD4&WWI

General Procedure for Generating Charts

The MS Excel program makes charts from the spread sheet automatically when you select adjacent rows and columns containing the data you wish graphed. If the data to be graphed is not in adjacent rows and columns, generating the chart is a little more complex, but still straight forward. An excellent tutorial for making Excel charts is found on website: http://psdam.mit.edu/rise/tutorials/excel/excel3.html

I will give you a short tutorial on how to make a chart using data from an Excel Worksheet. I will show you *how to do it* using two examples:

- Creating an OEX & DJIA chart from adjacent columns B&C over the last 6 month time period of 2005. The *Date* is in *column A* for all of the charts.

- Creating an OEX & WWI chart with the OEX in column B and the WWI in column G for the same time period of 2005.

The first procedure summarized below assumes the columns containing your data are in adjacent columns:

Cover the adjacent columns starting with the Row having the column Titles. Hold *Ctrl* down and move the cursor over the column titles. Continue holding Ctrl down and move the cursor down to the row of the first data. Continue holding Ctrl down and hold the right button of your mouse dragging down to cover all the rows with cells containing the information you want displayed graphically. By starting with the row containing the titles, then these titles will automatically appear on your graph or chart. Next click on the *chart wizard icon*, select chart type from the list of charts.

Assume we select Line Chart. Next select subtype. Assume we select lines with points for data. Then click on next. You will see a picture of your chart. Click next to get a picture of the chart with legend, select position of legend. Assume you select right. Now the chart has the DJIA curve at the top of the Y-axis and the OEX near the bottom. What we need for a good chart is to have the DJIA on a second Y-axis.

Click next and we get step 4 of the chart wizard which has two options: an object on the worksheet or a new sheet for the chart. Assume we select new sheet and enter a name for the Chart: OEXDJIA6moChrt. Next click on Finish, even though we do not like the appearance of the chart. We can customize the chart to look acceptable from the finished chart on the OEXDJIA6moChrt sheet. Fig 8.10 below is what the chart looks like before the trimming steps.

Figure 8.10 OEX & DJIA 6 Month Chart

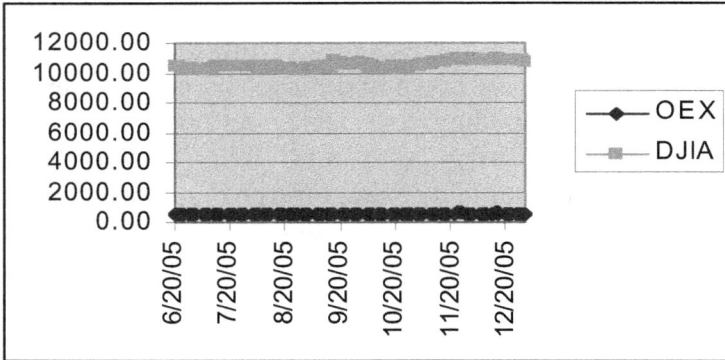

Here are the trimming up steps to take:

Add a second Y-axis for DJIA. Place the cursor on the DJIA curve and right click. You will receive a menu box, select *format data series.* Select *plot series on secondary axis.* This will create a second axis for DJIA, which makes a much better chart with the lines for the OEX and DJIA much closer together as show in Fig 8.11 below:

Figure 8.11 OEX & DJIA with 2nd Y-axis for DJIA

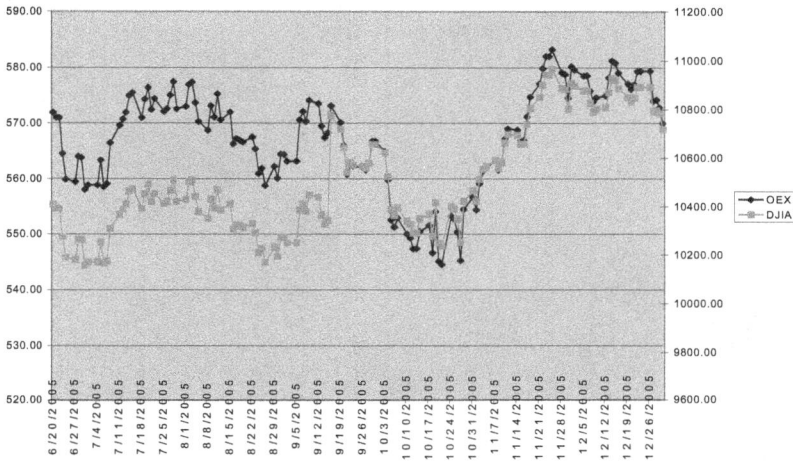

The final trimming steps: Add Chart Title, Title the left and right Y-Axes, adjust the Y-Axis scales to better fix the variations for the two indices, adjust the orientation of the dates and date format on the X-axis and finally set the background color to light green. The trimming steps can be made by right clicking on the chart and selecting the background color, enter Chart Title, select Y axes and select OEX for the left Y-axis and DJIA for right Y-axis. Also right click on the Y-axes, select format axis, scale, and select the maximum and minimum values you want. Finally click on the X-axis, select alignment and rotate the dates to be 45 degrees for easier reading, select number type for the date. I prefer the format *4 Jan 05.* After all of the trimming, the final chart is shown in Figure 8.12 below and was placed on a new sheet:

Figure 8.12 Final Trimming of OEX & DJIA Chart

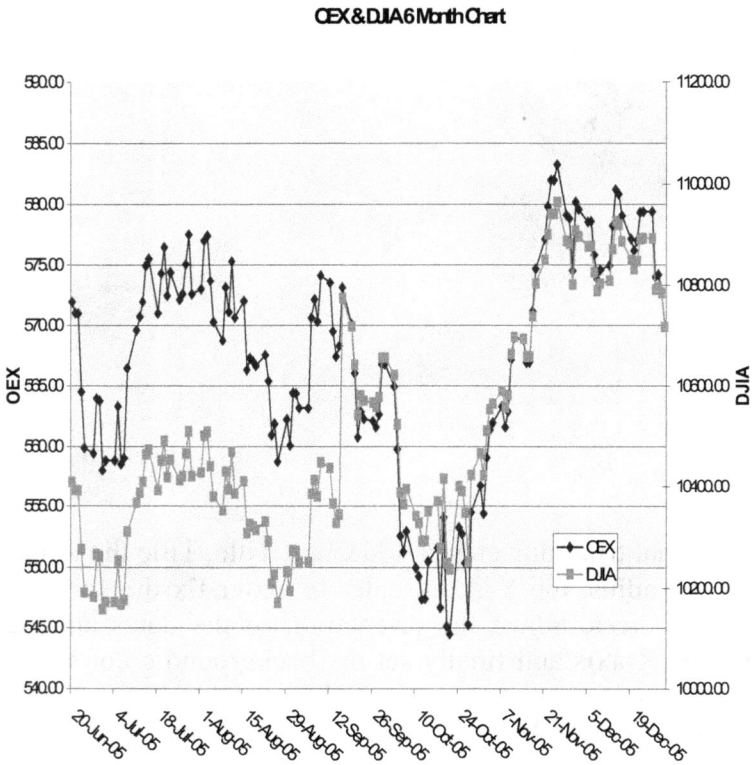

OEX & DJIA 6 Month Chart

You can make the chart part of the spread sheet with the data or create a new sheet for the chart.

You can add other features to the chart such as Trend Lines from a selection of trendlines such as linear, exponential, moving averages, etc. In the second example below I will show how to add the Linear Trend lines for OEX on the OEX & WWI chart. The steps are similar to those of the first example, but here the data columns are separate, OEX in Col B and WWI in Col G

After generating the chart using the chart wizard and going through the same trimming steps as the first example and adding the OEX Linear trend line, the chart appears as in Fig 8.13 below:

Figure 8.13 OEX & WWI with Linear Trend Line

OEX & WWI Last 4 Months 2005

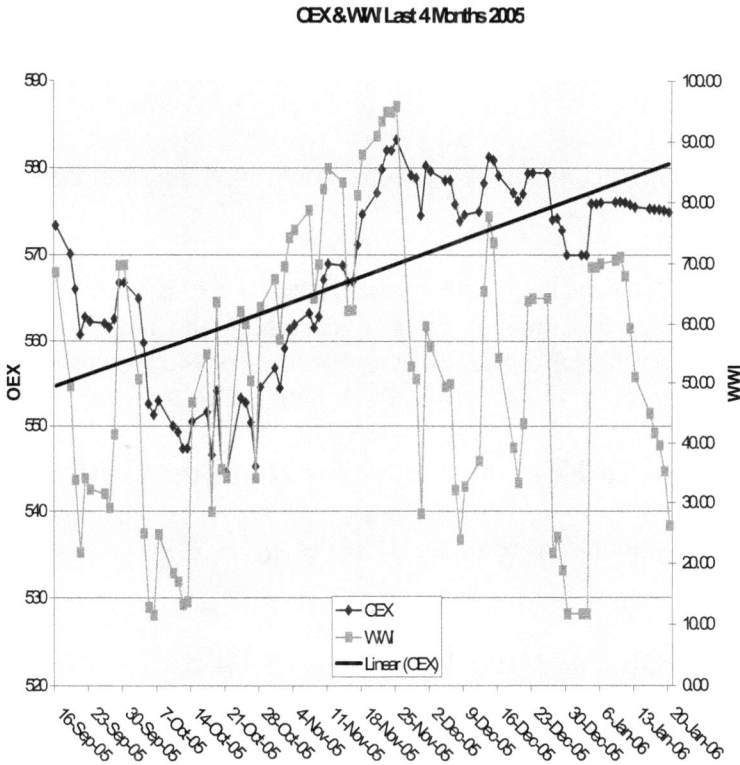

Details on How To add trend lines: Click on the curve for which you wish to add a trend line. For example ***right click*** on OEX curve. A box will pop up that has a box to select the series, OEX & WWI , to add a trendline to OEX, c lick on OEX. The same pop up has the following under the selection ***Type*** with the following trendlines available for selection:

- Linear
- Logarithmic
- Polynomial
- Power
- Exponential

- Moving Average – which has a box to select the period of the MA from 2 days to 90 days

These selections allow you to customize the chart to your personal desires for trend lines.

I hope this short tutorial will help you create your own charts from the Excel spread sheets available from the author described in his Self Adaptive Options Trading packages described in Appendix A.

How to Analyze the Structure of an Excel Chart

You may take any existing Excel chart and use the chart edit features to add features such as trend lines of the various types listed above, and moving averages Bollinger-Bands, etc.

How to Edit the Chart for the Next Options Month

Right click on OEX series, in the series box above the chart will appear:

=SERIES(VarOEXwwi!$B$3,VarOEXwwi!$A$4:$A$94,VarOEX wwi!$B$4:$B$94,1)

- Click on A$94 and change to A$114 the row number for Feb Expiration Date
- Click on $B94 and change to B$114

Right click on WWI series, in the series box above the chart will appear:
=SERIES(VarOEXwwi!$G$3,VarOEXwwi!$A$4:$A$94, VarOEXwwi!$G$4:$G$94,2)

- Click on A$94 and change to A$114
- Click on G$94 and change to G$114

After these changes the chart will now show the OEX & WWI curves for the Feb expiration. The important thing about these changes is it permits you to update your charts from the current Option Month to the Next Option Month. I normally make these chart editorial changes after market close on Expiration Friday.

After making these Chart changes the updated chart will appear as in Figure 8.14 below:

Figure 8.14 OEX & WWI Chart Updated for New Month

OEX & WWI Last 4 Months 2005

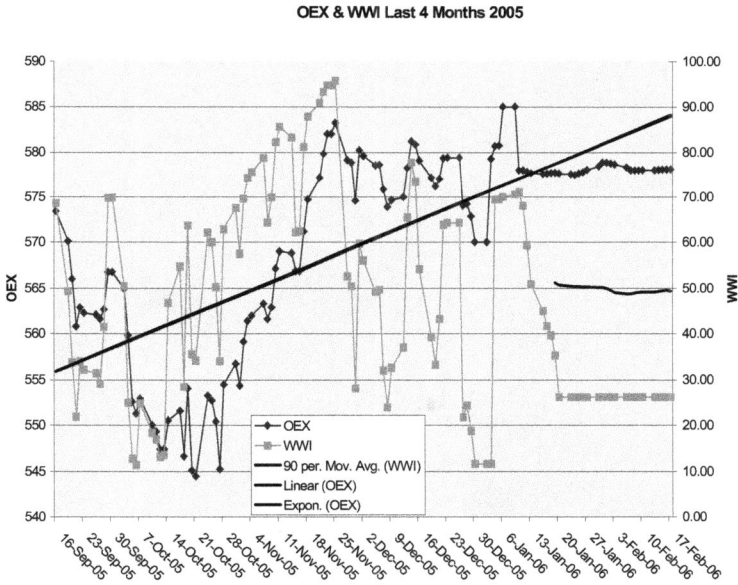

Dr. Jon Schiller

Part 2 Spread Sheet Tools for Index Options Trading

Chapter 9 Market Indicators to Identify Major Market Changes

The most difficult task in index option trading is deciding when a major market change has occurred. Chapter 4 described the strategies to use to profit from big changes in the market using the Moving Average Difference, MAD, and the Moving Average Divergence Convergence, MADC, charts. These charts were described as tools to help you decide when to switch from the basic short credit spread strategy to a combo spread with a long Call for Market jumps or a long Put for market plunges. If you make the wrong decision, it can cost you thousands of dollars. If you make the correct decision you can convert a potential loss into a gain of several thousand dollars.

One problem with the market indicator charts, such as the MAD and the MADC, is to decide which parameters to use in generating the chart. The MAD has only one parameter: the length of the moving average. The MADC has three parameters: the lengths of the long and short moving averages and the length of the smoothing difference of the 2 moving averages.

A third market indicator based upon a Genetic Algorithm is the MADCw (weighted MADC) which will be described later in this chapter. FastTrack, the company that specializes in charts and a trading system for Mutual Funds, has an excellent document that describes a number of market indicators and how to select the parameters for several indicators used for Mutual Fund Trading. Unfortunately the parameters FastTrack parameters are not optimum for OEX options trading and the FastTrack proprietary indicator AccuTrack is not applicable to OEX trading, since it is oriented to showing differences between a mutual fund and the SPX & DJIA. The OEX is too closely correlated to both the SPX and DJIA for AccuTrack to be a meaningful market indicator for OEX option trading.

Neural Network Trend Indicator Using 5 Market Signal Indicators

Using my Software, SelfAdapSigIndicOEX, I have adapted a three layer Neural Network using several of the OEX market indicators which shows significant changes in the trend of the OEX shown in Figure 9.1 below:

Figure 9.1 FeedForward Neural Network				Output>10 Uptrend		Output>10&<10 Dirediorless		
5 Input, 3 Layer, 1 Output				Output<10 Downtrend				
OEX= 5512	del=000			28 Sep 08 12245 OUTPUT				
Mkt Sig	Input	Wtg2	Layer1	3	Layer2	Wtg3	Layer3	Dntrnd	Uptrnd
Mad4	325	063911	205865	033333	069	10	1722	0	1	Layer 3
Mac94	163	038597	063018	033333	021		0	0	Strong
MACC	099	25	247428	033333	082		0	0	Very Strong
Sto%K%D	000	001655	0	033333	000		0	0	Subject to Rapid Reversal
VW	5956	0							

If layer 3 >10 OEX has an Uptrend. If later 3<10 OEX has a Downtrend. There are 4 layers of strength to indicate the level of Up or down trend.

38 Month Period: 20 Nov 02 to 20 Jan 06

The 38 month period is particularly interesting in that there was a large Rise and then a period of remaining high with large fluctuations.. *How well did the Neural Network Trend Indicators (NNTI) work during these 38 month changes for the OEX credit covered short spread?*

This period with the OEX and the NNTI are shown plotted in Figure 9.2 below with the UpTrends shown as the tall bars and the DownTrends shown as the short bars:

Figure 9.2 Neural Network Trend Indicator

Neural Network Indicator

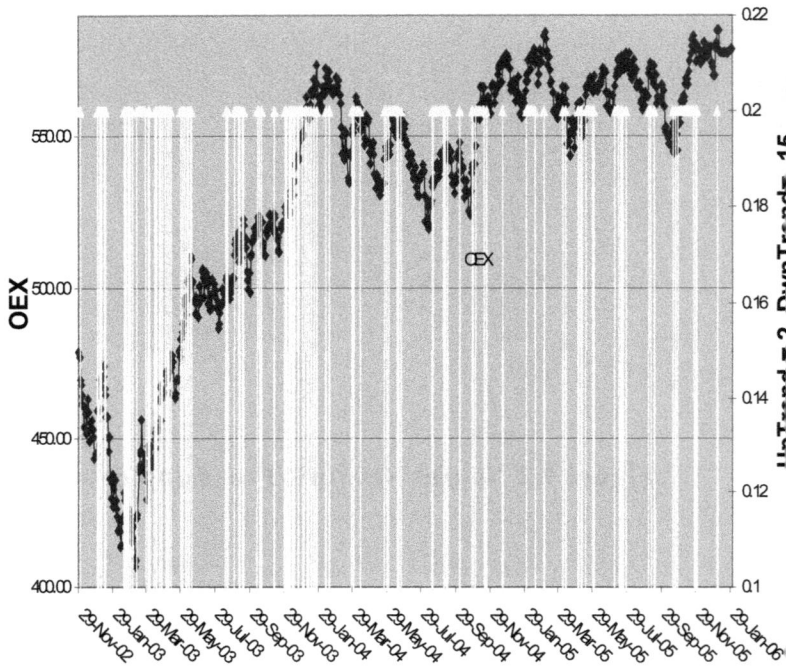

Nov 2002 to Mar 2003 Plunge & June 2003 Recovery

The one day plunge of over 14 points on the 24th of January 2003 was disconcerting because it revoked memories of the 1987 crash, but it was neither as deep nor as long. The OEX is shown for the period before and after the plunge in Figure 9.3 below during which period it had a 1-day jump of 14.07 on 13 Mar 03 followed by another 1-day jump of 14.57 2 trading days later making a 3 day rise of almost 30 points. As may be seen from the chart there was a recovery from the low of the period to the end of period on 17 Jun 03 of over a 100 points. As may be observed from the chart below the NNTI does a good job of indicating the trends during this 6 month period.

Figure 9.3 Neural Network Down Trend Indicator (NNDTI) Nov 02-Jun 03

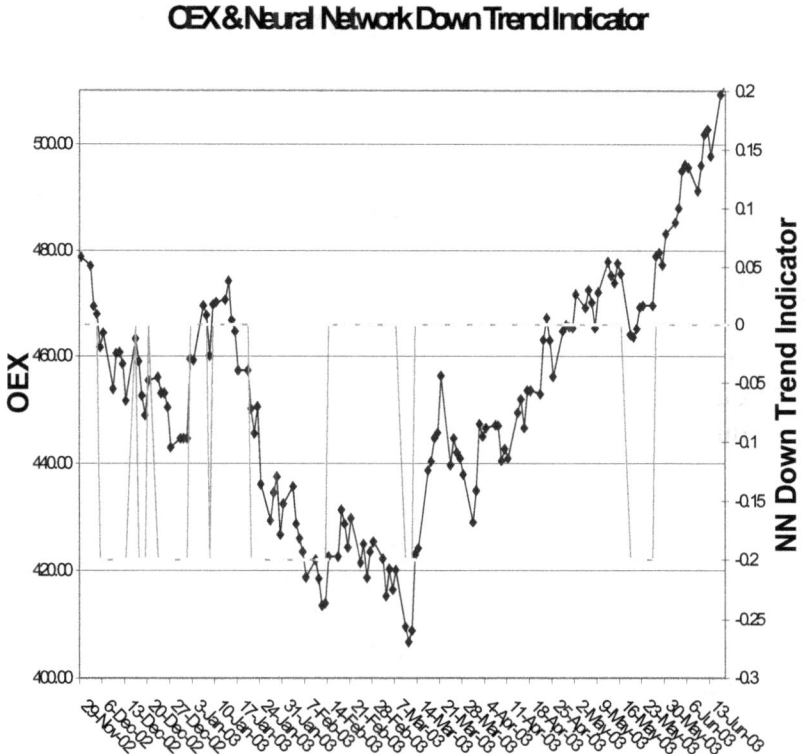

OEX & Neural Network Down Trend Indicator

How well does the Down Trend Indicator work during this same 6 month Period? The NNTI Down Trend Indicator is shown in Chart 9.3 above. The down trend indicator does a good job of predicting **Down Trends** over this 6 month period that had some large drops and recoveries. For example:

1. During the beginning of the Dec 02 plunge the down indicator showed a down trend by showing -0.2 on the chart, which on the NNTI spread sheet is shown by a -1 of the NNI 5 input, 3 layer output.

2. During the Jan 03 to Feb 03 drop, the down indicator showed a -.2 on the chart or -1 on the NNI output.

Period Aug 2005 to Jan 2006: Drop & Recovery

During this time period the OEX dropped 33 points the beginning of Aug 05 and recovered 39 points by Nov 25th 05 until it finally threatened to break through the 590 level in Jan 06. Below in Figure 9.4a for the Neural Network *Up Indicator* and Figure 9.4b for the *Down Indicator.* Again for this more recent 6 month period the Neural Network Indicators do a good job of showing the Trends. Figure 9.4a shows a steady up indication during the Nov 05 recovery and more wobbly up indications during the Sep 05 and Jan 06 smaller recoveries.

Figure 9.4a shows the Neural Network Up Indicator below is the plot for the 6 month period between Aug 05 and Jan 06. Figure 9.4b shows the Neural Network Down Indicator for the same 6 month period between Aug 05 and Jan 06. Both charts are below.

Fig 9.4a Neural Network Up Trend August 2005 Thru January 2006

Fig 9.4a OEX & Neural Network Up Trend Indicator

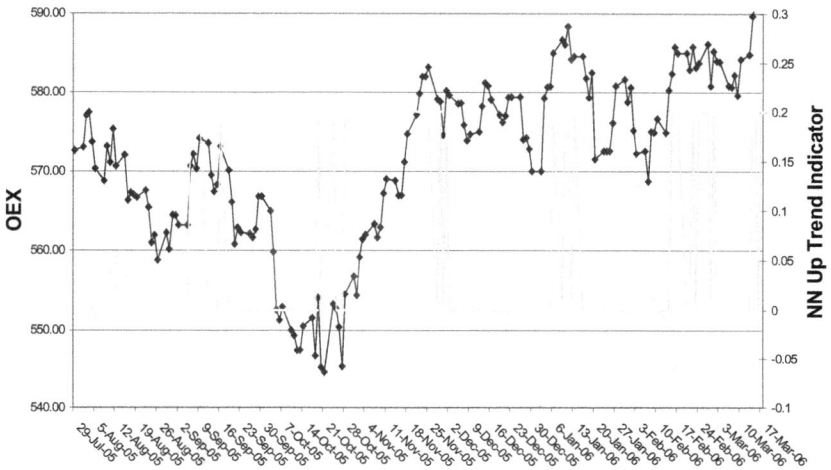

Fig 9.4b Neural Network Down Trend August 2005 Thru January 2006

Fig 9.4b OEX & Neural Network Down Trend Indicator

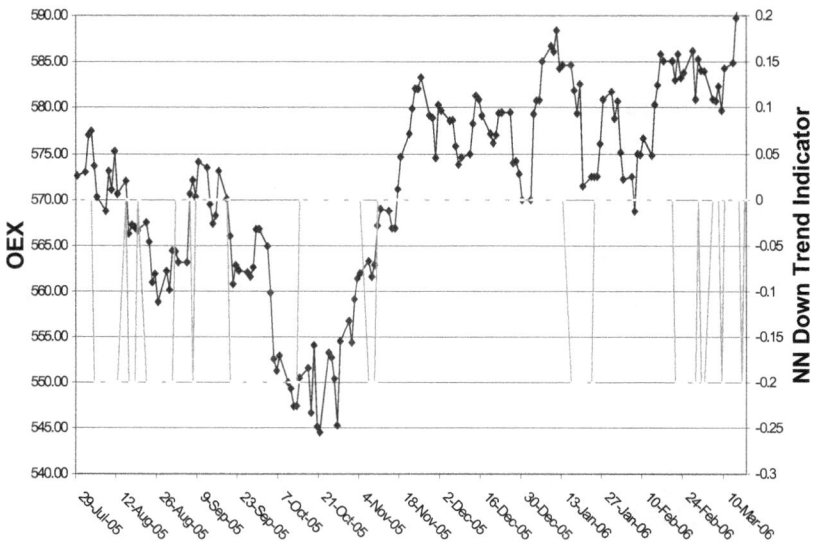

The MADC Chart from SelfAdapSigIndicOEX ending Jul Option Month 2008 is shown in Figure 9.4c below:

MADC & OEX

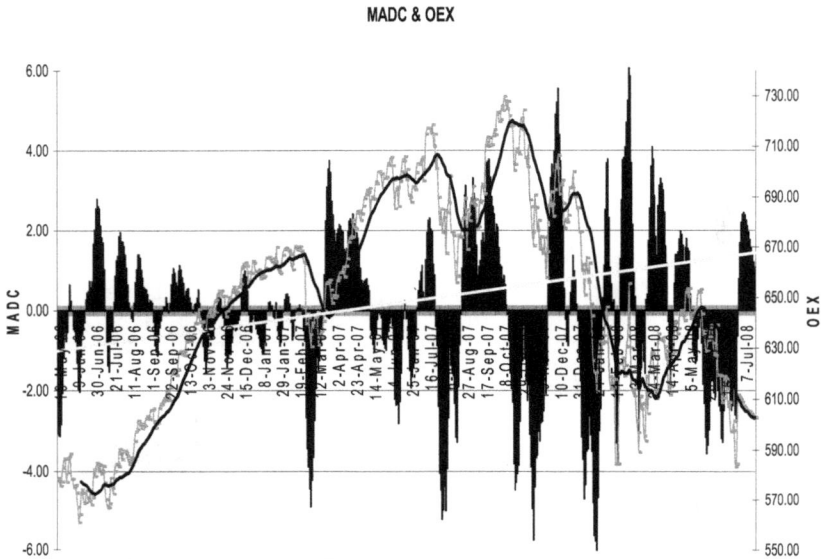

The Down Indicator is shown for the same 6 month period in Figure 9.4c above. As may be seen in the chart, the down indicator shows -.2 on the chart (***Down Indication***) during the May 08 to Jul 08 slide, and intermittent indications when the OEX traveling from 525 up to 730 in Nov 07 to 580 in Jul 08.

In summary I find the Neural Network Up and Down Trend Indicators useful to keep track of the mood of the OEX market:

- Up Trend
- Multiple Up Trends
- Down Trend
- Multiple Down Trends
- ***No Trend***

I check the Neural Network output on my software SelfAdptSigIndOEX daily to see which of these three indications are shown as I update the software, which is a 30 second task. I believe it gives me a view of the market indications I have been tracking now for a couple of decades, but now have the trend indicated by combining the Mad4, Mad9-4, MADC, and Stochastics %K-%D signal indicators. It shows the trend but does *not* provide a trigger like the Welles-Wilder Indicator (WWI) does for my Currency and Options Trading. So I include the WWI on the NeuralNet sheet of this software. This way the Neural Network sheet shows when the WWI signals an strong Up movement: WWI<20 or Down movement: WWI>80.

Some Major Market Moves during the Last Decade & Half

Some of the older major moves from the 1987 Monday Market Crash and the 1990 Gulf War Plunge to the Spring 1994 volatility will be described briefly below. Perhaps we can learn some things from considering some of these big changes in the OEX during more than 2 decades.

1.   **1987 Market Crash:** This market crash was fortunate for Short Spread traders since it occurred the Monday after Options Expiration Friday. I observed this crash while I was living in Spain and trading in London. I awaited until the end of the week of the crash to open a 2 sigma Covered Credit Short Spread (CCSS). The premiums were unusually large so the Initial Credit was larger than usual for the new option month.

2.   **October 1989 Market Plunge:** This one day 20 point mini-crash in the OEX occurred on 12th Oct 89 and an 8 point recovery the next day. None of the indicators gave an early warning of the plunge, it was too abrupt. But all three indicators switched from positive to negative the next day after the plunge. The indicators told you what you already knew!

3.   **Gulf War Plunge 1990:** The OEX reacted by dropping sharply when the 1990 Gulf War exploded during the late summer 1990. During the period from 19 Jul 90 thru 23 Aug 90 the OEX dropped from 350 to just over 290, a drop of 60 points. The 3 indicators switched from positive to negative the same day and stayed negative during the long drop.

4.   End of Gulf War Recovery, Jan-Feb 1991: The recovery at the end of the Gulf War began on 8 Jan 1991 with the OEX at 292 and continued until it reached 350 by the 13 Feb 1991; a rise of 58 points in 5 weeks, over 10 points per week. All three indicators turned positive at the beginning of the Feb 91 option month. So had you followed the market indicators and opened a Feb 90 Combo Spread (Long Call, Short Put), then you would have profited from a 40 point rise in the OEX during the Feb option month.

5.   January 1992 Market Jump: The next major market move was during the Jan 1992 option month when the OEX moved from 363 to 392, 29 points during the option month. All three market indicators indicated a rise at the beginning of the Jan 92 option month. A Combo Spread (Long Call, Short Put) would have earned a nice profit.

6.   Spring 1994 Plunge, Recovery & Fall Back: The March 94 to June 94 time period is particularly interesting since it showed a big drop, a big rise and then another big drop all in the period of 3 months. *How well did the indicators work during these traumatic changes for the OEX short trader?* The 3 indicators charted with general agreement during this time period.

7. OEX Chart Figure 9.5 below shows a Downward Trend Line from May 07 thru Jul 08. The OEX slid from 730 in Oct 07 thru Mar 07 when it hit a 690 low. Then the OEX climbed back to 650 in May 08 and then dropped rapidly to less than 570 during the Jul 08 expiration week as may be seen in the Chart of Figure9.5 below.

Figure 9.5 OEX & WWI May 07 Jul 08

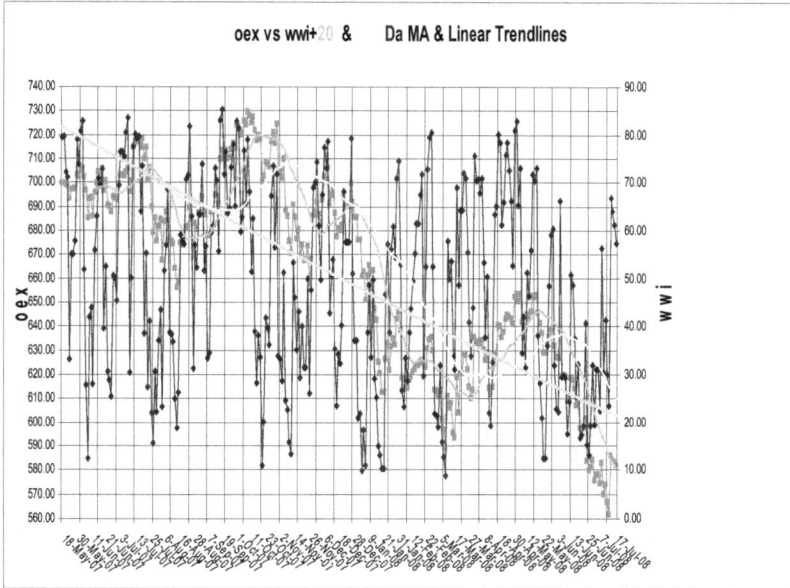

As may be seen from the OEX chart Figure 9.6 below the OEX had a steady rise from 1983 through 2008, except for the Oct crash of 1987 shown as a sudden small drop on the logarithmic scale chart. By the beginning of 2000 the OEX reached almost 800. Then after hanging around 800 point until Fall of 2000. The OEX begin sagging until mid 2002 when it bottomed out until it began a steady rise up to April 2006 when the OEX hit a 4.5 year high. Then the details of the decline until Expiration week of Jul 08, shown in more detail in Figure 9.5 above. Another interesting feature show by the 25 year chart of the figure below is that the volume grew from a small value to over 6 billion. This high volume is the reason we use OEX for options trading!

Figure 9.6 OEX & Trading Volume for 25 Years

```
S&P 100 INDEX (OEX)                              Splits: ▼
as of 11-Jul-2008
```

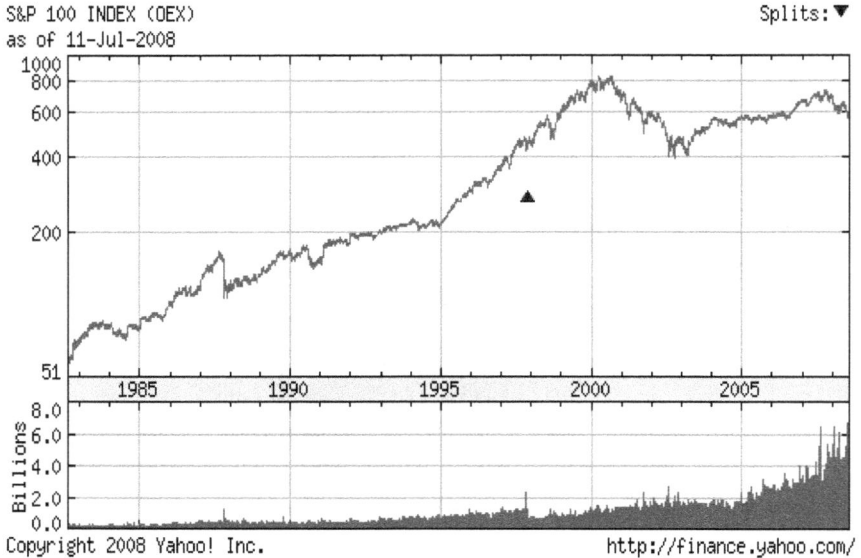

Score Card for the 3 Market Indicators for Rises and Falls

• October 89 Mini-Crash: The drop was too sudden and too short lived to benefit traders from the market indicators. All 3 signaled the drop at close of the day it happened. So the indicators were accurate, but not very helpful to OEX trading strategies.

• Spring 94 Correction: All 3 indicators gave an early warning, but the real warning of the Apr 94 drop was in the magnitude of the indicators rather than a change from positive to negative. This type of indication is difficult to interpret. So three indicators got a C- for signaling the start of the big drop.

• Spring 94 Recovery: All 3 indicators gave warning, the MADC gave the best signal

• June 94 Fall Back: The MAD gave the best signal of the new drop, MADC was two days late.

- Beginning of the Gulf War Plunge: All three indicators gave an accurate warning of the start, so all get an A+.
- End of gulf War Rise: All three gave an accurate signal of the recovery so all get an A+.
- January 92 Jump: All three gave an accurate signal of the recovery so all get an A+.

The MAD has the highest correlation with the OEX. So if you are going with a single of these OEX Signal Indicators, such as computed by my SelfAdapSigIndicOEX software package, MAD is the best and is easiest to compute using the 30 day exponential average.

I have found over the last several years that the Welles-Wilder Indicator is the best for giving an easy to interpret indication:

- WWI> 80 signals the market is overbought and is ripe for drop
- WWI<20 signals the market is oversold and is ready for a rise

The 2 sigma Cover Credit Short Spread is profitable 90% of the time. The market signal indicators give false signals many times so moving a threatened CCSS when either the short Call or short Put is threatened may not be wise, and a switch to a Combo Spread may not prove profitable. *Remember the 2 Sigma Covered Credit Short Spread is the best strategy to use to produce a continuing stream of monthly profits to make your Trading Capital Grow.*

As OEX Weeklys mature which expire each Fri, I would add weekly credit spreads opened as a parallel strategy to the monthly 2 sigma spreads, to increase monthly income without adding to risk. Typically 5 weekly condors can yield a weekly profit of $500 for a margin of $2500 open on Thu and expire Fri.

Part 2 Spread Sheet Tools for Index Options Trading

Chapter 10 Guide to Market Indicator Charts

Keeping track of the market on a daily basis is an important task in option trading. In this chapter we are going to examine several types of charts to help tell which direction the market may move based on past movements and their patterns and see how spread sheets can generate the charts. We have already evaluated several market indicators in Chapter 8 with parameters and the correlation between signal indicators. Chapter 8 also showed a Neural Network combination of 4 Signal Indicators: The Mad4, MADC, MAD9-4, and Stochastics %K-%D to show an Up Trend, or Down Trend. Chapter 9 evaluated historical charts for OEX showing index movements over the last 25 years and an OEX Chart with emphasis over the last year of the market.

Moving Average Difference, MAD

The MAD is the simplest to compute market indicator, and in general is the most responsive to a change in the market direction. The single parameter for the MAD is the number of days in the moving average. However, there are two ways to compute the moving average:

1. The simple moving average
2. The exponential moving average

I use both, but if you want to see changes in the MAD for different numbers of days, for the moving average, then the exponential moving average is easiest to change.

The workbook SelfAdapSigIndicOEX.xls , which generates several of these indicators: MAD, MADC, MAD9-4, Stochastics %K-%D, Bollinger Band, and WWI, uses the exponential moving average to facili11tate the change. My

SelfAdapDTN4.xls workbook computes the WWI for the OEX, SPX, 14 stocks, and one high return Mutual Fund (FLATX) also uses the exponential moving average (7 day) to compute the WWI for these underlying stocks & indices.

Moving Average Divergence Convergence, MADC

The MADC is a chart widely used by technical analysts and is an excellent market indicator for changes in direction of OEX. It is computed as follows:

1. Compute 20 day exp Moving Average = Mad20
2. Compute 10 day exp Moving Average = Mad10
3. Compute the difference between the 20 day & 10 day moving averages = Mad20-Mad10 = Mad(20-10)
4. Compute the 13 day exponential moving average of the Mad(20-10)

To compute the Exponential Moving Average it requires today's data and yesterday's data to compute two factors F1 & F2 using N the number of days:

- $F1 = 2/(N+1)$
- $F2 = 1-F1$
- N Day Ex Moving Average = OEX(today)*F1 +OEX(yesterday)*F2

My SelfAdapSigIndicOEX workbook uses 6 columns to compute the MADC: column B containing OEX and columns H thru K computing the 4 items above, and finally L for computing the MADC.

Genetic Algorithm Weighted MADC or MADCw

A more complex signal indicator was described by Casimir Klimasauskas[1] used Genetic Algorithms (Gas) to develop a weighted MADC called MADCw, based upon 6 moving averages varying from 2 days to 40 days, and 5 simple MADCs with 5 weighting constants. I have used the MADCw in workbooks I used when I lived in Spain, but no longer use it because of the complexity of the computing and the lack of benefit compared with using the WWI for making trading decisions for opening Long Calls or Puts or for Buying or Selling Lots or Currency.

Welles-Wilder Indicator, WWI

The Welles-Wilder Indicator, WWI, varies between 0 and 100 and is based upon the up and down differences in the OEX or other underlying equities. These differences are smoothed by an exponential smoothing function (same as for the exponential moving average). The spread sheet SelfAdapDTN4.xls generates the WWI for the OEX, SPX, 13 stocks and FLATX Mutual Fund. When the WWI is greater than 80, this indicates the market is overbought and is vulnerable for a drop, which is a trigger for opening a Long Put. When the WWI is less than 20, this indicates the market is over sold and ready for a rise which is a trigger for a Long Call. The 5 Equations for computing WWI are below

Column C   =IF((B565-B564)>0,B565-B564,0)
Column D   =IF((B564-B563)<0,B564-B563,0)
Column E   =E563*0.75+C564*0.25
Column F   =F563*0.75+D564*0.25
Column G   =100*(E564/(E564-F564)) = WWI

Figure 10.1 OEX WWI

---

[1] Genetic Algorithms Build a Better Market Timing System, Winter 94 Issue, AI in Finance, by Casimir C. Klimasauskas

Date	OEXXO	Up	Down	Up7daexMa	Dn7daexMa	WWI
16-Jun-06	572.76	0.00	-1.41	2.56	-2.03	55.74
19-Jun-06	568.53	0.00	-4.23	1.92	-2.58	42.65
20-Jun-06	568.72	0.19	0.00	1.49	-1.94	43.44
21-Jun-06	573.71	4.99	0.00	2.36	-1.45	61.94
22-Jun-06	570.82	0.00	-2.89	1.77	-1.81	49.45
23-Jun-06	569.47	0.00	-1.35	1.33	-1.70	43.93
26-Jun-06	572.29	2.82	0.00	1.70	-1.27	57.22
27-Jun-06	567.83	0.00	-4.46	1.28	-2.07	38.15
28-Jun-06	570.88	3.05	0.00	1.72	-1.55	52.57
29-Jun-06	582.20	11.32	0.00	4.12	-1.16	77.97
30-Jun-06	579.56	0.00	-2.64	3.09	-1.53	66.84
3-Jul-06	584.74	5.18	0.00	3.61	-1.15	75.86
4-Jul-06	584.74	0.00	0.00	2.71	-0.86	75.86
5-Jul-06	581.79	0.00	-2.95	2.03	-1.38	59.48
6-Jul-06	584.16	2.37	0.00	2.12	-1.04	67.09
7-Jul-06	580.62	0.00	-3.54	1.59	-1.66	48.83
10-Jul-06	581.60	0.98	0.00	1.44	-1.25	53.50
11-Jul-06	583.68	2.08	0.00	1.60	-0.94	63.05
12-Jul-06	576.96	0.00	-6.72	1.20	-2.38	33.46
13-Jul-06	570.08	0.00	-6.88	0.90	-3.51	20.39
14-Jul-06	567.32	0.00	-2.76	0.67	-3.32	16.87
17-Jul-06	566.62	0.00	-0.70	0.51	-2.66	15.94
18-Jul-06	568.35	1.73	0.00	0.81	-2.00	28.87

The WWI is computed for some 22 underlying equities in SelfAdapDTN4.xls software package.

The above Figure 10.1 is particularly interesting because it shows the OEX WWI = 16.87 on 14 Jul 06 (oversold) & WWI = 28.87 heading back up, 18 Jul 08, expiration day, just 2 trading days later. A typical up and down movement of the OEX.

The Workbook that computes the market signals for OEX at the present time is SelfAdapSigIndicOEX.xls which your author provides for free to anyone purchasing his other Software: SelfAdapDTM4.xls, SelfAdapFutOp.xls or SelfAdapCur. The 18 charts included in the Signal Indicator workbook include:

- NeurNet3yrUpTrend

- NeurNet3yrDOWNtrnd
- NeurNet6MoUpTrnd
- NeurNetUpLst6Mo
- NNDnTRNDLst6Mo
- ChartMad9-4
- ChartMadc
- ChartStochastics%K-%D[1]
- ChartCumDel
- Chart3OEXBollingerBand
- ChartOverBotOverSld (Welles-Wilder[2] Indicator & Bollinger Bands)
- ChartStochastics&WWI
- ChartMADC&WWI
- ChartMAD9-4&WWI
- ChartMAD4&WWI
- SAMNCandlestickChrt
- RSIvsOEXChrt

I keep these charts updated daily and update the charts time period on Expiration Friday of each month. This workbook book, includes the Neural Network shown in the NeuralNet sheet of this workbook.

References:

1. "Double-Smoothed Stochastics", William Blau, Technical Analysis of Stocks and Commodities, Vol. 9 No. 1, (Jan. 1991. [/ 42) Other references to the stochastics indicator ore cited in this article.
2. "New Concepts in Technical Trading Systems", J. Welles Wilder, Jr., Trend Research, Greenboro, NC, (1978)

Part 3 Spread Sheet Tools for Decision Making

Chapter 11 How to Use Decision Charts during Option Month

Spread sheet generated charts are a great help in visualizing what is happening during a 4 or 5 week option month. Remember the options expire on the third Friday of the month and normally a new covered credit spread position is taken on Monday after expiration   or at least during the first week after expiration. *My Monthly Update Service is $120/yr.* So the first task of the new option month is updating the charts and spread sheets used to evaluate the short credit spread during the course of the up-coming option month. The charts to be updated include the *Surveillance Charts* as well as the *Decision Charts*. Normally the charts are updated after close on expiration Friday and the spread sheets are extended to go beyond the next expiration Friday. You now have your surveillance and decision tools ready to face the challenges of the market for the new option month.   Then you may feel comfortable opening a new short credit spread after open for the month. Please note: *I use a 20 day extrapolation algorithm to predict the market values in the future.*

Surveillance Charts for OEX Index Option Trading

The OEX & WWI chart with the 200 day and 20 day moving averages and the linear trend line is excellent for showing the overall market variation and the trend. It also shows any oversold or overbought conditions as indicated when the 7 day WWI is penetrated at the level of 80 (overbought) or 20 (oversold). This chart is shown in the chart of Figure 11.1 below:

Figure 11.1 OEX & WWI with Trendline & Moving Avgs

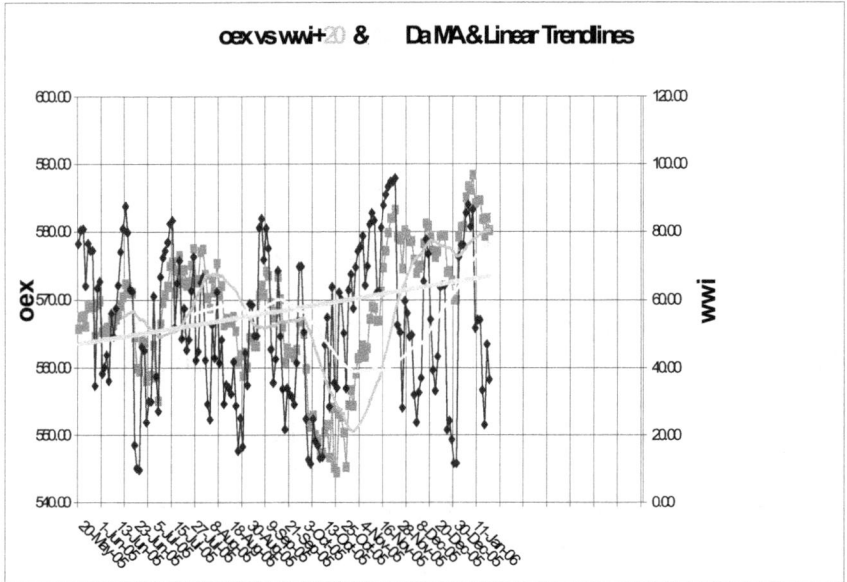

oex vs wwi+20 &   Da MA & Linear Trendlines

As may be seen in chart of Figure 11.1 above the trend for the OEX is up since the linear trend line has a slight upward slope 1.25 points per month. As may be seen the Min is 544 and the Max is 588 or a del = 44 or an average of 5.5/month. Also you may see the WWI>80 level was penetrated from 20 May 06 thru 11 Jan 08, 7 times or on the average, once per month. The WWI<20 level was penetrated 5 times or once each 1.6 months.

Remember a penetration of 80 is a trigger to open an ATM (at-the-money) Long Put, since WWI>80 is a signal that the OEX is going to drop. As may be seen the WWI >80 reliably predicted a big drop, so a Long Put would have made a good return on cost in one or two days.

A penetration of 20 is a trigger to open an ATM Long Call, since WWI <20 is a signal that the OEX is going to rise. Again the Long Call could have been closed out at a nice profit after 1 or two days, as may be seen from Figure 11.1 above that the OEX indeed did jump after the WWI dropped below 20 on only 1 or 2 days.

So the nice thing about Figure 11.1 is it provides both a *surveillance chart* of where the OEX is going and a *decision chart* showing the WWI triggers for opening a Long Call or Long Put when the WWI is <20 (Long Call) or WWI is >80 (Long Put).

Market Indicator Charts: Where is the Market Going?

The MAD, MADC, and WWI market indicator charts are generated using the spread sheet: SelfAdapSigIndicOEX.xls workbook. The charts are generated in this workbook and as discussed earlier in Chapter 8, the 5 input 3 layer Neural Network is generated in this workbook to show the *Up or Down trend* of the OEX.

The charts generated by SelfAdapSigIndicOEX.xls workbook have been shown in earlier chapters and will not be repeated in this chapter. So to be a successful Options Trader, become accustomed to using the surveillance and decision charts to:

- Note when the market is moving in an exaggerated manner that may require protective changes to your threatened Short Call or Short Put of your open Covered Credit Short Spreads.

- Note when the WWI has triggered a Long Call or Long Put position allowing you to add profit to the Initial Credit of your 2 sig Covered Credit Short Spread. You must watch the market during the 4 or 5 week Option Month to assure that the Initial Credit received when you opened the CCSS becomes profit at expiration, without having to take corrective action to protect an ITM short Call or Put.

Part 3 Spread Sheet Tools for Decision Making

Chapter 12 How to Enjoy Overall Trading Profits & Yet Suffer Occasional Losses

I've had about 3 times that the OEX market has had big plunges:

1. *In Oct 87 when the market crashed on Monday after the 3rd Friday expiration.* My covered credit short spread (CCSS) position had expired worthless leaving the Initial Credit received when the CCSS was opened as profit. After a week or so after the crash, it was safe to enter the market again, using the normal 2 sigma CCSS positions to generate the monthly profit. This had been a worrisome crash since it occurred almost exactly 58 years since the 1929 crash.

2. *When the first President Bush started the 91 Gulf war against Iraq for attacking Kuwait.* As I recall I had a large loss that month. You must be prepared for a loss about once per year. It's part of Options Trading.

3. *On Expiration Friday of Jan 06 I had a Put CCSS using Google (goog) as the equity.* I had received a nice Initial Credit when that goog CCSS was opened. On Tue of Expiration Week the CCSS was valueless, meaning if I had closed the position I would had the original Initial Credit as Profit. However Thu 19 Jan 06, the US Justice Department announced it was attacking Google for not providing their large DATA Base. This caused goog to plunge 36 points the next day on Expiration

Friday placing my short Put in the money. It happened quickly and I was not clever enough to close the position at the beginning of the day. As a result instead of earning 3 points credit, I lost 10 points (the difference between the Short Put strike price and the Long Put strike price. *A New Rule (endorsed by other Options Analysts: When a Covered Credit Short Spread reaches zero or <0.1 during the option month, Close the position to assure the profit.*

I updated my 2 sigma computations for OEX the day after Jan 06 Expiration.   It is unlikely for OEX to be affected as a single stock can. OEX dropped 11 on that expiration day, but my CCSS finished worthless, meaning my original Initial Credit became Profit.

Here are the OEX 2 SIGMA computations: Monday OEX sC590/LngC595 and sP555/LngP550 are indicated as 2 sigma CCSS positions in Figure 12.1 below:

Figure 12.1 C590/595 & P555/550 the last period being Sep 08

101.5%	**6 Mo**	**OEX 2SIG = 29.04**
176.4%	**3 Mo**	**OEX 2SIG = 30.63**
Use	**13 Mo**	**OEX 2SIG = 40.02**
	Average 3 Periods	**33.23**

The reason I use OEX 2 SIG Covered Spreads is that the probability that the OEX will remain within the 2 sigma limits, and therefore safe, is 90%. Sorry, I can't guarantee 100% safety, that can only be guaranteed by a savings bank account.

Please find below in Figure 12.2 the results I have achieved using Welles-Wilder Indicator (WWI) triggered Long OEX Calls or Long OEX Puts over 3 years.

Figure 12.2 Three Years of WWI triggered Long Calls & Puts

Total Prft	**Avg Prft/Trd**	
$30,460	**$622**	**46 #Trds**

The strategy: buy an at-the-money (ATM) Long Call when WWI<20 and buy an ATM Long Put when WWI>80. I use this strategy to augment the profits from the OEX CCSS monthly positions.

During early 2006 the 2 sigma Call CCSS received about 0.6 or 0.7 points, and the 2 sigma Put CCSS received about the same, so the Initial credit would be about 1.3 points for the Condor. If you were trading 10 options, the Initial Credit = 10*100*1.3 = $1300 less Comm. The margin = 10*100*5 = $5,000. So the return on Margin = 26%/month or over 300% per annum. Such high potential allows occasional losses and still double your capital per year.

The most you could lose if the OEX rose or dropped outside your short Call & Put limits is the width of the spread (5 points) times the number of options times 100. Or if the OEX moved outside the 2 sigma limits, *and you took NO protective moves,* then for 10 options Max Loss = 5*10*100 = $5000 or 3.9 months profit.

So for a worst case analysis, assume one loss per year, the annual profit would be:

$1300*12 Initial Credit - $5000 Loss = $10,600. You could increase this annual profit if you took corrective action like closing the threatened spread and opening a new spread at a safer distance from the market.

Sorry, unexpected happening such as Bush's first Iraq war and the Justice Department's attack on Google can't be predicted. You must learn to suffer an occasional loss.

I have 3 software packages at $70 each:
1. SelfAdapDTN4.xls, covers OEX, QQQQ, SPY & 13 Growth stocks
2. SelfAdapFutOp.xls covers some 11 Futures & their options
3. SelfAdapCur.xls covers Euro, Brit Pound, Swiss Franc & Yen uses WWI to determine when to buy or sell a Lot of Currency. One Lot is about $100,000 value and requires $1000 margin to open a Lot. I trade only 0.2 lot requiring only $200 mgn.

4. I also provide SelfAdapSigIndicOEX.xls free to anyone who orders any of the first 3 packages; it includes charts for MAD, MADC, MAD9-4, & Stochastics%K-%D. This also includes a Neural Network sheet that uses the above signal indicators to indicate and Up or Down trend of the OEX market.

These software packages can be ordered from me by email: jonsch1@verizon.net and sending a check to:

- Emilie Smyth
- 701 E. Pine Ave #118
- Lompoc, CA 93436
- USA

If you would like an electronic version of the book with colored charts, please send $50 to Emilie as above.

Two Sigmas for OEX Next Option Month

I update the 2 sigmas to use for the next OpMo (option month) during the *last week of the options month* to get an idea of what Initial Credit I will receive when the new OEX CCSS is opened. The table of Figure 12.1 shows the computed 2 sigmas for the last 13 month, 9 months and 6 months as well as the average of these 3 values. In general the 2 sigmas increase with decrease in the number of months used for computing the 2sig, but in no regular fashion. It is important for you as an Index Option trader to update your 2 sigma computations at the end of each option month, as I do in my SelfAdapDTN4.xls workbook.

In order to compute how much I may receive with the new OEX CCSS position, during the last week I take advantage of the CBOE OEX options chain found for free on their website: http://www.cboe.com/DelayedQuote/QuoteTable.aspx

To use this chain enter OEX in the box, click on *all Options,* then click on *Submit* to get the Chain to appear on your

screen. I have a sheet in SelfAdapDTN4 called CBOECmdCntr
where I paste the data copied from the CBOE sheet using the *copy
special, text* command under Edit of Excel. Since I had already
computed that ShrtCall590/LngC595 & ShortPut555/LngP550
were the 2 sigma Call & Put strike Prices for the next option
month, then I copy the Call and Put strike prices around these
values and paste them in the Excel worksheet where I store this
data, which is updated each time I obtain a more recent reading.
The view of this OEX Call data is showed in Figure 12.3a below:

Figure 12.3a CBOE OEX Call Premium Data

Calls	Last Sale	Net	Bid	Ask	Vol	Open Int
06 Feb 585.0 (OEB BQ-E)	2.4	-3	2.4	2.45	2807	2499
06 Feb 590.0 (OEB BR-E)	1.3	-2	1.25	1.4	3583	5176
06 Feb 595.0 (OEB BS-E)	0.7	-1.1	0.65	0.75	2211	5461
06 Feb 600.0 (OEY BT-E)	0.4	-0.55	0.4	0.45	1134	8484
06 Feb 605.0 (OEY BA-E)	0.25	-0.3	0.2	0.3	957	5153

The view of this OEX Put data is showed in Figure 12.3b
below:

Figure 12.3b CBOE OEX Put Premium Data

Puts	Last Sale	Net	Bid	Ask	Vol	Open Int
06 Feb 540.0 (OEB NH-E)	1.3	0.9	1.3	1.4	701	4227
06 Feb 545.0 (OEB NI-E)	1.6	1	1.35	1.75	3245	2522
06 Feb 550.0 (OEB NJ-E)	2	1.25	2	2.1	2785	2920
06 Feb 555.0 (OEB NK-E)	2.7	1.7	2.4	2.85	1287	2531
06 Feb 560.0 (OEB NL-E)	3.7	2.35	3.7	3.8	1834	4587

So to compute the 2 sigma Call & Put Initial Credit
assuming 10 options, the equations are given below:

Call590/595 Initial Credit = 10*100*(1.3-0.7) = $600 less
commission

Put550/545 Initial Credit = 10*100*(2.7-2.0) = $700 less
commission

***The total Initial Credit* = 600+700 = *$1,300 less
commission***

At TradeKing if the double spread, or Condor is opened, the Commission for 10 condors = 4.5+10*.65*4 = $30.50, so you may see, a commission less than 2.5% of your initial credit.

How much Margin would be required to open this Condor (2 sided CCSS) positions?

I recommend having twice the amount in your brokerage account than the computed amount needed for Margin. This policy will avoid unnecessary margin calls from your broker. Again assuming 10 options the margin computations are:

Call Margin = 10 *100*5 = $5000, since the OEX spread is 5 points between the short Call and Long Call. *Note: this is also the maximum amount you could lose for an adverse movement.*

Put Margin = 10*100*5 = $5,000
Condor Margin = 10/100*5 = $5,000

My policy then is to have a minimum of $10,000 in your trading account to make this trade, or 2 times the margin.

TradeKing considers opening both sides of the credit spread an Iron Condor, and only requires the margin for either side to open both sides. This is the same policy the LON broker had when I lived in Spain.

So What Percent Return Do You Receive on Your Margin?

%Return/Margin = $1300/$5000 = 23.6%/Mo = 284% per annum.

Note: the return on Capital would be $1300/$10,000 = 13%/Mo =156% per annum

Out-Month Strategy for Threatened Short Credit Spread

If you take corrective action for a threatened Call or Put Covered Credit Short Spread and the expiration is less than a week, it would probably be wise to close the threatened position and open a new CCSS in the next option month. This would mean the closed out position would probably be less than the new position due to the decay of premiums during the option month. So the options of the current month would have decayed relative to the options for the new option month. The Jan 2006 option month would be a good example to use since the OEX plunged 11 points on Expiration Friday of that month. Assume the following parameters for this example:

1. On Thursday before Expiration Friday the OEX = 582.51 at close

2. Our open Put CCSS: short Put 575 = 0.3 Long Put 570 = 0.2 CCSS Value = 0.3-0.2 = 0.1

3. It appears that our P575/570 is safe and will expire worthless making our initial 0.7 points received as profit for the Option Month, therefore no action is taken.

4. On expiration Friday the OEX opened down at 581.8 still safe for the short P575. However the OEX started a steady slide downward. A half hour after market open the OEX = 580, still safe for the short P575, but worrisome.

5. At an hour an half after market open the OEX = 577.5, only 2.5 points above our short P575, increasing the worry. *Should we take corrective action? NO! Wait and hope for recovery.*

6. Two and a half hours after market open the OEX dipped below 575 making the Short P575 In-the-Money before recovering above 575 momentarily. *Decision: Close out the Jan P575*570 and open a Feb 2 sig P555/550!*

What Does it Cost to Make this Protective Change?

The premiums for the Jan Put covered spread at the time of close out of the P575/P570 are: P575 = .40 & P570 = 0.1 the cost for 10 Options = 10*100*(0.4-0.1) = $300 +comm.

The premiums for the new Feb Put Covered spread at the time of Open of the P555/550 are: P555 = 2.7 & P550 = 2.0 so the Credit for the New Put CCSS = 10*100*(2.7-2.0) =$700-comm. So the net credit of the protective change = $700-$300 = $400 – commission

Long Put Strategies Using Out-Month OEX Options

The high premiums for out-months suggest some strategies to augment your in-month short spread profits. One such strategy would be to use the out-months Chaos Pattern strategies described in Chapter 3. How would the *first two day long Put strategy* have worked for the Feb 2006 option month: At Friday 20 Jan 05 Expiration for Jan 06 options, OEX closed at 571.51 at a drop of -11.0, it would appear wise *NOT* to open the *first two day long Put* for the Feb 06 option month. It was wise to take no Put position since the next two days the OEX rose 1.01 point so the ATM Put at Strike Price = 570 would have declined causing a loss instead of a profit.

How about the Previous Option Month on 16 Dec 05, the Expiration Friday, the OEX closed at 579.08 down 1.77 points. Buy 10 Jan P580 to Open at a premium = 6.8 at close on 16 Dec., at a Cost = 10*100*6.8+comm = $6,831 Then Sell 10 Jan P580 to close at market close on 20 Dec with the OEX = 576.19 (*drop of 2.89 in the first 2 days*) at a premium = 7.3. So the *profit in using the first 2 days Chaos pattern = 10*100*(7.3-6.8) –Comm = $500-$62 = $438, the %Return on Cost = 438/6831 = 6.41%.* So you may see the first 2 day Put strategy does yield a profit, but you must avoid using when a huge expiration day drop occurred such as the 11 point plunge on the Jan 06 Expiration Friday.

Figure 12.4 below shows the SelfAdapDTN4 Trading Center for the August 2008 option month during the last week of the July 2003 option month. Please note that the C605/610 & P535/530 condor are shown for the Jul OpMo and the 2 sigma August Condor of C600/605 & P520/515 are shown which show an Initial Credit = $1268 for the upcoming month. This spread sheet shows a monthly return on Margin of $5000 as 13.56%, which is typical return for OEX.

Figure 12.4 OEX Credit Spreads for Sep OpMo, Last Wk OpMo   Huge Drop caused by Investment Bank Restructuring

SelfAdapDTN4 Trading Center

	SPX 1,229.93	Date	15-Sep-08	ATM Longs	Prm Got	Prm Now
0.9 566.93		NOPS =	2	C655	11.91	9.90
OEX Del -10.78		Comm =	$11.60	P655	11.09	7.60
OEX DTN Options			TK Cap =	$18,214	Mgn%Cap =	
566.93	-10.78	2Sig	40.02		$39,584	After OEX Trade
CNDR NOPS = 10		NOPS =	2	OEX/SPX	SPX Del	StkPrice
2SigCall	605	2SigPut	525	0.46	-21.77	42.95
OEX Crdt Spreads		Total =	$328	Condor Expir	QLD	15-Aug-08
P555/565 Wkly						
C580/585 Wkly						
C630/635	0.35	-0.05	$328	$376	#DIV/0!	$328
C635/640	0.35	0.05	$328	$276	$966	$0
P545/540	0.66	0.70	$638	-$66	$210	#DIV/0!
C625/630	0.34	0.10	$318	$32	$5,000	
Expir 18 Sep		Total =	$956	-$34	19.12%	%Ret/Mn
Sep 08 2SIG COVERED SPREADS		Today =		15-Sep-08	23.00	$4,623

Monday 15th Sep 08 was a tumultuous market at open caused by reshaping of Lehman Brothers Holdings Inc. and Merrill Lynch & Co. made by details negotiated on Sat & Sun before or a forced sale to Bank of America for $50 billion in stock and more ominously, American International Group Inc. is asking the Federal Reserve for emergency funding. The world's largest insurance company plans to announce a major restructuring Monday.

The swift developments are the biggest yet in the 14-month-old credit crises that stems from now toxic subprime mortgage debt

To give you an idea of how rapidly options can change from Friday to Monday: for a condor that was

1. On Fri the Sep Condor: C625/630 = 0 P545/540 = 06, or closed at a total of 0.6

2. on Mon 3 hours after market open: C625/630 = 0.8 P545/540 = .05 for a total = 0.85

This dramatic example shows how week-end news can affect the Monday market. It is another good reason to use the rule: When either the Call spread of a Put spread of an OEX condor reaches zero, then close the null value spread.

Part 4 Internet Aids and Tactics to Increase Profits

Chapter 13 Some Websites to Give Data for Options and Currency Trading

This chapter tells you how to use the WINDOWS program I developed to help manage my options trading. As I grew more experienced in trading, I extensively modified my original program and rewrote it in Microsoft's Excel Macros which use Visual Basic programming code. I now copy the Watchlist quotes from DTN.IQ for Indices and stocks and *paste special, text* in OpQte2 of SelfAdapDTN4 for updating my OEX and other 14 or more underlying equities. I copy the currency quotes from Mgforex & enter the data into SelfAdapCur using a macro initiated by CntrlX.

Overview of SelfAdapDTN4.xls

To run the *SelfAdapDTN4.xls* find the file and double click to open. I normally use the DTN.IQ Watchlist for the data to feed the above software package. The OpQte2 sheet allows you to enter the real time quotes during the trading day from the Watchlist. Remember: DTN.IQ, website: http://www.dtniq.com/ After subscribing to this service they provide an access symbol for obtaining a watchlist portfolio and OEX chains and realtime charts.

I prepare this Watchlist for the portfolio used during the current trading month. Normally I use the same portfolio for the whole 4 or 5 weeks of the Option Trading Month. However, I normally make adjustments in the Options quoted during the month on the Watchlist.

Also for trading OEX Weekly options, I have 4 lines at the end of the DTN portfolio for entering the 2 Call options and 2 Put options for the weekly Call and Put spreads. As I explained earlier I use the strategy of opening the weekly OEX credit spreads either Thu or Fri of the option week for which the options expire at options closure on Friday of the weeks that have weekly options.

Of course the 4 weekly OEX credit Call & Put symbols change weekly during the option month for the 2 sigma OEX condors.

This SelfAdpDTN4 file contains a OpQte2 sheet for entering the watchlist portfolio realtime data, which updates SelfAdapDTN4 Trade Center sheet for controlling your option trading positions

1. Computes the Real Time Profits or Losses for the ATM Long Call & Long Put positions as well as the OEX Credit Spreads

2. Computes and displays the Welles-Wilder Indicator (WWI) for the OEX & SPX & 19 stocks included in the Portfolio and tracked by separate pages in SelfAdapDTN4

3. Computes the monthly OEX Covered Credit Short Spreads (CCSS) & Condor for 12 growth stocks. ***This is the most valuable function of the Trading Center sheet.***

4. The OEX, SPX, and some 19 stocks are linked and the WWI computations are updated for these 2 index options, 19 or so, stocks. (I modify the stocks tracked from time to time.)

5. The Charts are updated for these 21 underlying equities for the realtime quotes.

6. Sheets are provided for OEX, SPX, GOOG and other stocks for entering the CBOE options chains during the trading day 15 minutes delayed or after market close. These option chains can include all of the options for the current month, the next month and as many months in the future you may have an interest. The OEX & SPX CBOE options chains also include the weekly option chains and the Leaps.

7. Access to these CBOE option chains is obtained free from website:

http://www.cboe.com/DelayedQuote/QuoteTable.aspx

As a matter of interest, I normally open the DTN.IQ real time Portfolio website at the beginning of the trading day, and refer to it as many times as I am concerned or interested during the trading day, and after close of the trading day. I open the CBOE delayed quote website during the day when looking for data to open a new position or at the end of the trading day for the OEX, SPX, and any stock I may have an interest in. *I have checked the correlation between DTN.IQ and CBOE and have found them to correlate closely.* Also DTN.IQ provides selectable Option Chains and Charts for near realtime reference during the trading day. I normally overlay these Chains and Charts on the SelfAdapDTN4 Trading Center sheet for easy reference.

Open New OEX Short Credit Spreads: Condor

I normally open new OEX Call & Put covered credit short spreads on the first Monday after the monthly options expiration date, 3rd Friday of the month. However, if the market is acting strangely during the last week of the option month or the OEX WWI is >80 or <20, you might wish to wait a few days to see if the market is becoming more normal before opening the new Call & Put CCSS. For example at close on the 3rd Fri of Jun 08, the OEX WWI= 17.93, so I waited to see if the OEX bounces back from it's recent slump before opening a new Iron Condor for Jul 08 option month. I use the real time quotes and the computations of my SelfAdapDTN4 trade center covered spreads for entering my double sided CCSS order into my broker's website. You need to enter the following data for the new OEX CCSS:
- Underlying Equity: OEX & whether a Call or Put, assume Call
- Number of Options: Let's assume NOPS = 10

- Strike Price to Sell to Open spread: Let's assume Call 590
- Strike Price to Buy to Open spread: Let's assume Call 595
- Enter the Credit desired for the new CCSS: Let's assume Credit = 0.7
- Then Click **Enter Order** and check your broker's website for Spread Orders to make sure you have your order Sell 10 OEX Call 590 & Buy 10 OEX Call 595
- To open both Call and Put spreads simultaneously you may open an Iron Condor which requires entering the number of spreads, in order from the lowest to highest strike prices symbols, and the credit you wish to receive for the Condor. TradeKing condor entry form automates this process and makes it easy to do.

Assuming your order was entered as you expected, *log off* your brokers website and wait for a time to make sure your SelfAdapStkOp *OpCmdCntr* sheet say you should have received the CCSS order filled based on your Realtime Interquote Portfolio quote. *I find it interesting when using the OEX chain display when I see the number of spreads I asked for appear on the chain, meaning I see my trade being made.*

Now your OpCmdCntr sheet should compute the Initial Credit you received for opening your new Call CCSS as: *Call Initial Credit* = NOPS*0.7*100 − Comm = 10*0.7*100 - 3.5*10*2 = $700 −$70 = *$630*.

Your OpCmdCntr sheet also computes the Margin required in your broker account for the CCSS position you opened: Margin = NOPS*(Strike Price difference)*100 = 10*(595-590)*100 = 10*5*100 = $5,000.

Your OpCmdCntr sheet also computes the %Returned on Margin = $630/$5,000 = 12.6%

If you opened a 2 sigma Put Covered Spread, you would repeat the procedure above for the Put side of your two sided CCSS, which will be shown below:

- Underlying Equity: OEX & whether a Call or Put, Now enter Put
- Number of Options: Let's assume NOPS = 10
- Strike Price to Sell to Open spread: Let's assume Put 545, symbol = OEY IE
- Strike Price to Buy to Open spread: Let's assume Put 540, symbol = IF
- Enter the Credit desired for the new CCSS: Let's assume Credit = 0.6
- Then Click **Enter Order** and check your broker's website for Spread Orders to make sure you have your order Sell 10 OEX Put 555 & Buy 10 OEX Put 550 or the Iron Condor order it you use this order technique. *Note: you are more likely to receive individual credit spreads rather than an Iron Condor because of market executing factors. I still recommend using the Condor order procedure.* Note: if you place the Call and Put spreads separately, once both are executed, your account gets credit for a Condor, meaning the Margin required is only half as much as a Put Spread or Call Spread alone were opened.

Assuming your order was entered as you expected, *log off* your brokers website and wait for a time to make sure your SelfAdapStkOp *OpCmdCntr* sheet say you should have received the CCSS order filled based on your Realtime Interquote Portfolio quote. *I find it interesting to note on the DTN.IQ OEX Option Chain, that I often can see my order get executed in real time by seeing that the number of options I am requesting show up in the number of pips (volume).* I have confirmed this fact several times by going back to TradeKing and observing that my spread order was indeed executed.

Now your OpCmdCntr sheet should compute the Initial Credit you received for opening your new Call CCSS as:

Call Initial Credit = NOPS*0.6*100 − Comm = 10*0.6*100 - 3.5*10*2 = $600 −$70 = *$530*.

Your OpCmdCntr sheet also computes the Margin required in your broker account for the CCSS position you opened: Margin = NOPS*(Strike Price difference)*100 = 10*(555-550)*100 = 10*5*100 = $5,000.

Your OpCmdCntr sheet also computes the %Returned on Margin = ($630+$530)/$10,000 = 11.6%

So now you have a two sided 2 sigma OEX CCSS, or Iron Condor, opened for the new Options Month. If the OEX stays below the short Call = 590 and above the short Put 545, then your Initial Credit of $1,160 becomes the monthly CCSS profit as the both sides of the spread become worthless at 3rd Friday Expiration.

Open a Growth Stock Credit Spread

There are two types of growth stock Credit Spreads that I consider opening during the Options Month:

1. 2 Sigma GOOG Put Credit Spreads. Since 24th March 2006 GOOG was added to the S&P 100 Index which has stabilizes this growth stock as a potential high premium Put CCSS. For example on 24 Mar 06 the GOOG = 369, for a Put CCSS with shortP350/longP340 = 1.9 premium difference the, *Initial Credit* = 10*100*1.9 -29 = $1,871 for a Margin = 10*10*100 = $10,000 for a %Return per Margin = 18.71% or a per annum return = %224.5.

2. When a growth stock such as AAPL has a Welles-Wilder Indicator (WWI) < 20, or AAPL has a new product introduction such as 14 Jul 08, then open a *near the money* Put Credit Spread for a high premium Put CCSS. For example when AAPL = 173.88 with a new product , then 5 August spreads: 1shortP165/LngP170 = 2.25 premium difference, for 5 spreads, the *Initial Credit* = 5*100*2.25 -29 = $1,096 for a Margin = 5*5*100 = $2,500 for a %Return per Margin = 43.84% per month or a per

annum return = %526.   Aug 08 Symbols for AAPL: Short Put 170 = APV TN, Long Put 165 = APV TM

3. As may be seen by these two growth stock Credit Spread Examples, a higher % Return can be obtained with these Growth Stock Credit Spreads than the more conventional OEX 2 Sigma CCSS for OEX which typically has a % Return per Margin = 13% for the option month.

4. As a follow up to the AAPL LngP165/sP170 did later: on 28 Jul the AAPL = 157.68, *meaning corrective action would need to betaken, since the short P170 was in the money by over 12 points.* So these spreads using less than 2 sigma are risky.

Dr. Jon Schiller

Part 4 Internet Aids and Tactics to Increase Profits

Chapter 14 Option Brokers with Automated Website Trading

I have been doing automated website trading for almost a decade. In 2006 I decided to do some website research to find the best available website brokers for option trading. I was looking for the lowest commissions and the best automated services. I found the website brokers using the Google Search Engine. I have used several website brokers now, and have found the one discovered by Google Search in Feb 2006 very satisfactory and the lowest commissions I have found.

TradeKing

TradeKing: www.tradeking.com/   has an excellent electronic trading platform for options trading. Their commission for 5 OEX Long Positions = $15.50 based on their April 2006 commission structure.

You may register for an account using the above website. Once registered with a user name and code word it is easy to use their *userfriendly* electronic trading platform. It is easy to open a trading account which can be done with just a Minimum of $2000 funding for covered credit spreads to become accustomed to using the trading website. It is easy to trade:

- Under the Trade Tab are the following selections
  - Options
  - Stocks + EFTs
  - Mutual Funds
  - Fixed Income
  - Order Status

So you may see this Trade Tab allows you to place an order for trades in the above categories.

If you would like to place a 2sigma OEX Covered Credit Spread, then click on Trade, select Option, then select Spread to obtain the trade form for opening a Covered Spread

- To Open an OEX 2sig Covered Credit Short Spreads start by clicking the **OPTIONS** Tab. Under that tab are the sub-tabs
  o Basic: Which is a form for opening or closing Calls or Puts
  o Covered Call
  o Spread
  o Straddle
  o Strangle
  o Combo
  o Butterfly
  o Condor
  o Collar
- Next click on the **Spread** Tab or **Condor** Tab

The Spread has provisions for entering the information needed for opening or closing a Spread. The Condor has the automated platform for using both the Put Spread and Call Spread. As I mentioned before, this automated platform requires entering the lowest strike price, which would be the Long Put and moving up to the highest strike price which would be the Long Call.

For example if you wished to open 10 OEX short Put 580/ long Put 575 credit spreads for a credit of 0.75, then you would enter into Leg 1: buy to open: OEB PP, Leg 2: sell to open: OEB PO; then enter 10 into the quantity for each Leg; finally select *credit* for obtaining the covered credit spread and enter the Limit of 0.75. To review what the order would be, click on Preview Order. The website has the nice feature of then displaying the amount Initial Credit you would receive if filled at the **Credit requested** and gives the Commission cost for the order. This brokerage has the lowest commission of any brokerage I have reviewed: $4.5 per trade plus $0.65 per option contract. So the commission for the 10 Call Covered Credit Spreads = $4.5 + 10*2*0.65 = $17.50. The commission for OptionsXpress would have been \$44.95 based on the commissions structure in April 2006.

The trade tab has a sub-tab for *Order Status* for providing the trader of this electronic website a summary of all open and executed orders and all trading activity in the account.

The tools tab has a means of computing the probability of staying below your Call spread's short Call and for computing the probability of staying above your Put spread's short Put. I find these probable computations are useful in evaluating how safe your spreads will be if opened, or how safe any opened spreads may be.

Tactic of Put CCSS of Growth Stocks with Short Put Close to Market

The availability of the low commissions of a broker such as TradeKing and the availability of Trading Advisors such as Premiumtrends permit the use of this tactic of opening a Put covered credit short spread (CCSS) on technical growth stocks with the short Put less than 2 sigma from the market. By using these close in short Puts you will receive higher initial credit, but at higher risk, since this type of stock tends to be unstable and market news can cause large drops in the market.   In May 06 Premiumtrends recommended a Put CCSS with a near to the market short Put.   I used Yahoo Financial and CBOE delayed quotes to obtain the premium information. Using such services as Premium trends is can be used for finding growth stock close-in Put Credit Spreads. Frankly, I prefer to use the growth stocks in my software, SelfAdapDTN4.xls, to provide surveillance on a number of growth stocks such as AAPL, RIMM, RIO, GOOG, DRYS, BIDU, and POT. Provide visual surveillance during the first week of the option, month, and select a close-in Put spread from one of these on the above list.   It is a risky tactic, but one for which large returns on you margin can be achieved.

Links to Trading Advisors *17 Advisors*
Listed below

A recent development in options trading is the automation of the trades within the boundary of parameters set by you such as number of options (NOP), % Return on Capital, % Utilization of Capital, or the % of available cash in your trading account. You may of course place your own 2 sigma CCSS for OEX to generate your steady monthly income, but the automated trades are made within the parameters set by you to take care of trading targets of opportunity to augment your CCSS income. These augmented profits may, of course, help off-set any losses caused by market threats to either the short Call or short Put of the CCSS due to corrective changes discussed in Chapter 1 (*So What Corrective Action Would Be Taken?*).

The author has evaluated a number of trading advisors who have links to one or more options brokers which permit the advisors' trade recommendations to be executed without intervention or participation of you, the trader. These trades are, of course, within the trading parameter limits set by you with your options broker. These limits can be changed by you at any time that an automated trade hasn't already, been executed. As you might expect, there are numerous pages of *fine legal print* that you must click *I Accept* the terms and conditions to protect the broker from any legal consequences in case a trade goes awry. As in most of these *legal terms and conditions statements*, the broker's lawyers are more protective of him rather than you. But you must accept the terms and conditions to use the automated services.

I believe these trading services which link the Broker's Executions based on the input from a trading advisor gives opportunity to make quick profits on the spare trading capital sitting in your trading account. These trading advisors have many different and proprietary means for coming up with *high win to loss options trades*. I am sure these advisors would be able to find more and faster such target of opportunity trades than you or I could since they have huge options data bases as resource to ferret out potentially profitable trades. Their claims in their literature about their advisory service is uniform:

- Low Loss Rate
- High Win Rate
- Large % Return on either Capital or Margin

For example, they often claim 10% to 20% Return on a Trade. For example, if a Long Call cost $2000, this would bring a profit of $200 to $400 using their typical claims.

I believe these **automated executions within limits** **(AEWL)** have some important advantages to we traders:

1. We can set up the trade parameters **a priori** during a calm period.
2. Using pre-set parameters will avoid those errors made by you, the trader, under the often rapid decision making for a real time trade.
3. Allow an entity with a larger data base to find potentially profitable trades than most of us with our limited data bases.
4. Many of these trade advisors promise to make a round trip trade in one or a few days, thus assuring a profit in a short time on the closed trades.

I believe that my program SelfAdapDTN4 which can insert the real time quote from DTN.IQ into the OpQte2 sheet and give real time snapshot of the OEX plus some 10 to 15 high tech stocks to find WWI triggered Long Calls or Long Puts comes closest to the resources these trading advisors use to find real time trades.

Some 17 Trade Advisors With Real Time Links To Brokers

I have researched some of the Trade Advisors available for real time links to OptionsXpress. You may explore the services provided by these many Investment Advisors below when there is a website included. Some of the advisors did not have a website that could be found using the Google or Yahoo search engines.

1. **Anacott Investments** http://www.anacott-investments.com/ The services provided by this

Investment Advisor can be explored on their website above. They specialize in LEAPS based on the Index Stocks QQQQ, DIA, SMH & HHH. Their target is 5% return on a trade.

2. **BigTrends**
http://www.bigtrends.com/sample.jsp?documentid= 95 This advisor's services can be studied by accessing their website. Big Trends specializes in profit-generating options strategies by identifying key trends in sector activity, trading volume, and volatility. They offer trading alerts and easy execution with daily trading guidelines.

3. **Day Trader Toad** http://www.daytradertoad.com/ specializes in OEX day trading. This advisor's services can be studied by accessing their website

4. **Deep in the Money**
http://www.deepinthemoney.com/home.html This advisor's services can be studied by accessing their website. Specializes in trading the QQQQs and also trades QQQQ options.   As I've explained, the QQQQ is a stock that *Represents the NASDAQ-100 companies.*

5. **Disciplined QQQQ Trading**
http://qqq.zarsby.com/ This advisor's services can be studied by accessing their website. It is another Investment Investor that specializes in QQQQ, QLD, and QID trading by provides two different types of alerts: An early morning alert service (10:15 AM EST) and an end-of-day alert service (5:45 PM EST). This Newsletter is for buying and selling QQQQ or Buying QLD instead of QQQQ or buying QID which is *emulated selling* of QQQQ. This is an example of a Newsletter that can linked to TradeKing for AutoTrade, in which you specify the dollar amount from your account that may be used for the automatic trade. This is for the underlying equities, NOT the options.

6. **The Dynamic Option Selection System**: Analyzing Markets and Managing Risk http://www.quirksmode.org/js/options.html This advisor's services can be studied by accessing their website.

7. **First Class** http://www.manta.com/   This advisor's services can be studied by accessing their website.

8. **Grand Slam Trading** http://www.trade-mentor.com/GrandSlam.html This advisor's services can be studied by accessing their website.

9. **Hamzei Analytics** http://hamzeianalytics.com/ This advisor's services can be studied by accessing their website.

10. **Insight Stock Picks** http://www.insightstockpicks.com/   This advisor's services can be studied by accessing their website.

11. **Investors Advisor** http://www.investmentadvisor.com/   This advisor's services can be studied by accessing their website.

12. **Kash Kings** http://www.kashkings.com/Disclaimer.htm This advisor's services can be studied by accessing their website.

13. **Liquid-Cash** http://www.liquid-00cash.com/ This advisor's services can be studied by accessing their website.

14. **Opening Bell Stocks** http://www.openingbellstocks.com/index.php This advisor's services can be studied by accessing their website.

15. **Option Principle** http://www.optionprincipal.com/   This advisor's services can be studied by accessing their website.

16. **The Optionist** http://www.theoptionist.com/ This advisor's services can be studied by accessing their website. They charge $700/year or $199.75/quarter subscription rate.

17. OptionSmart   http://www.optionsmart.com/
This advisor's services can be studied by accessing their website. Their Auto-trading with their partner brokerages available FREE of extra charge. They have offered auto-trading services since March 2002. and specialize in "high momentum" stocks with the strongest technical signals in order to "jump in and out".

Summary of Autotrade Advisors

As you may see from the summary of autotrade advisors given above there are several website brokers who have links to Autotrade advisors to do your options trading for you. For those of you who are adventurous and would be willing to trust others to make your trades for you automatically, you may be willing to try autotrade. Before doing auto trade you must do three things:

1. Chose a website options broker that offers the autotrade service.

2. Select a suitable autotrade advisor who has links to the options broker

3. Select the limits that the autotrade advisor can apply to your options account funds such as:

   • Value of Trade

   • Number of Options

Example: Autotrade Using Disciplined QQQ Trading one permitted by TradeKing: Must subscribe to Newsletter, A good way to augment your options trading profit by utilizing Autotrade

Disciplined QQQ Trading was founded by a Berkeley Ph.D. who began his modeling in 1994. The model has consistently beaten a buy and hold approach to investing by short term market timing utilizing exchange traded funds (ETFs). The NASDAQ 100 ETF, or QQQQ, provides diversification and is very liquid. Another form of the alert is to Buy QLD, which emulates Long QQQQ, when the alert is Positive; Buy QID, which emulates short QQQQ, when the alert is Negative.   The alerts are issued at 3:30 PM EST in order to allow for mutual fund trading cut-off times.

My experience with the QQQ Alert has been about $1000 per month for a Cash set aside for AutoTrade = $5000.

Part 4 Internet Aids and Tactics to Increase Profits

Chapter 15 Summary of Index Options Trading

This book has an objective of showing the reader how starting with a limited amount of trading capital that by using 3 strategies:

1. 2 Sigma OEX Covered Credit Short Spreads
2. WWI triggered Long Calls and Long Puts
3. Using Close in Growth Stock Credit Spreads

You can make your capital grow year by year even after suffering a monthly loss about once per year.

The following market signal indicators are useful in Index Options Trading:

- Welles-Wilder Indicator (WWI): <20 Up signal, >80 Down Signal
- Moving Average 4 Days (MAD4)
- Moving Average Convergence Divergence (MACD)
- Moving Average 4Da-9Da (MAD9-4)
- Stochastics%K-%D (STO%K%D)
- Neural Network OEX Market Trend combining MAD4,MADC, MAD9-4 & STO%K%D: Neural Network >10 is Uptrend, <-10 is Downtrend

The Welles-Wilder Indicator is used as a trigger for buying and selling options and currencies:

- When WWI > 80 this indicates market is Overbought and will Drop

- When WWI < 20 this indicates market is Oversold and will Rise
- WWI is a trigger for Buying Calls: < 20 or Buying Puts: >80
- WWI also is a trigger for Buying or Selling Currency Lots when <20
  or > 80

Strategy for Profiting from Short Term Variations in OEX

- When OEX WWI > 80, buy Long Puts
- After Long Put is Filled, Place order to Sell at 1 or 2 points more than paid for Put
- When WWI < 20, buy Long Calls
- After Long Call is Filled, Place order to Sell at 1 or 2 points more than paid for Call
- Typically Round Trip Trade takes 1 or 2 Days
- This WWI triggered Long Call & Put trading can add to CCSS monthly profits
- Chaos Patterns confirmed by WWI to open Long Put & Long Call Positions
  1. Long Put 1st 2 Days of Option Month: Open Mon after Expir, Close Tue
  2. Long Call 3rd Mon of Option Month: Open Mon of Expir Week, Close at Mon Cls
  3. Long Call Last 2 Day of Expir Week: Open Wed Expir Week, close at Fri Expir

  The probability of these Chaos Pattern strategies are increased by having WWI Confirm making the order

Example of Opening New Month's 2 Sigma OEX Covered Credit Short Spread

- Covered Call Credit Short Spread: short Call = Round((OEX + 2sig)/5,0), Long Call = short Call +5
- Initial Call Credit = NOPS*(sCprm-LCprm)*100
- Covered Put Credit Spread: short Put = Round((OEX − 2sig)/5,0), Long Put = short Put -5
- Initial Put Credit = NOPS*(sPprm-LPprm)*100
- Example: NOP = 10, 2 sig = 15.82, OEX = 575.31

- Call Spread: Short Call = 590, sCprm = 1.3, Long Call = 595 LCprm = 0.7 Initial Call Credit = 10*(1.3-0.6)*100 - 62 comm = $600-62 = $538
- Put Spread: Short Put = 555, sPprm = 2.7, Long Put = 550 LPprm = 2.7   Initial Call Credit = 10*(2.7-2.0)*100 -62 comm = $700-62 = $638
- Total Initial Credit for C590/595 & P555/550 = $1,176

Margin Required for OEX CCSS and the % Return = Initial Credit/Margin

- Margin = NOPS*SpreadWidth*100
- For example for the New CCSS example above:
- Call Margin = 10*5*100 = $5,000
- Put Margin = 10*5*100 = $5,000
- If both Call & Put Spreads are opened, the 10 Condor Margin = $5000
- Total Initial Credit = $1,176
- %Return on Margin = 1176/5000 = 23.5% per Mo or = 282.2% per annum
- Be Mentally Prepared for Occasional Loss

OEX 2 sigma CCSS for Aug 08 Option Month computed in SelfAdapDTN4.xls

- Segment of SelfAdapDTN4 Trading Center Sheet shown in Figure 12.4 Ch 12
- Showing OEX Covered Credit Short Spread for Aug 2008 option month
- The 2 Sig Call CCSS: sC600/LngC605, 10 Spreads
- The 2 Sig Put CCSS: sP520/LngP515, 10 S[reads
- The Call Crdt = $678, Put Crdt = $584
- For 10 OEX Condors, Margin = $5000 for the Condor
- The %Return on Margin = 13.56% per month, 150.7% per annum

The amount of premium received is 0.7 for the Call spread & 0.6 for the Put spread. A portion of the OpCmdCntr sheet taken on the 14th Jul 08 using Aug 08 options is shown in the figure 15.1 below:

AugC600/605	0.70	0.70	$678	-$26	$1,262	13.56%	
P520/515Aug	0.60	0.60	$584	-$26	$962	11.67%	-$52

This OpCmdCntr sheet of the SelfAdapDTN4.xls software package includes a OpQte2 sheet entering the entering of real time data from the DTN.IQ Portfolio during the trading day. The sheets for OEX, SPX, and 20 stocks have the WWI computed with each entry of real time data, permitting you to do day trading using the WWI triggered Puts & Calls for OEX & the 20 stocks. The 2 sigma values are also computed for OEX and the other indices and stocks.

Some Options Nomenclature

- 2 Sigma: two standard deviation for OEX or underlying Equity
- Short Call 2 Sigma above market means the probability of OEX rising above short Call is less than 10%
- Short Put 2 Sigma below market means the probability of OEX falling below short Put is less than 10%

Some Options Definitions

- An Option ATM (at-the-money) means it is a Call or Put option with Strike Price closest to the Market
- A Call Option OTM (out of the Money) means a Call with Strike Price Above the Market
- A Put Option OTM means a Put with Strike Price Below the Market
- Short Option is Sold & Long Option is Bought

A Welles-Wilder versus MADC chart is shown below in Fig 15.2

MADC & WWI

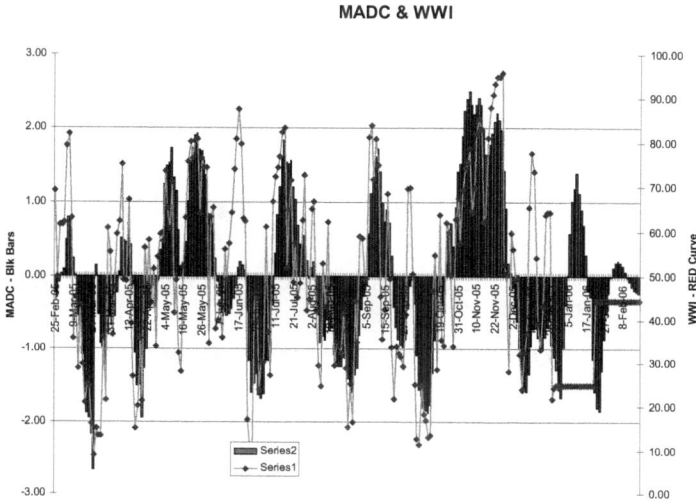

How to Make Your Capital Grow Using Index Option Trading

- This Assumes You begin with $14K in your Trading account
- First Mo You Have 6 Options for CCSS & 4 Options for Longs giving a Monthly Profit of $1160
- Each Mo you increase # Options from until on the 12 Month you have 14 options for CCSS & 8 options for WWI triggered LONGS
- Assumes One Month of Loss During Middle of year
- During last Month the Number options for CCSS = 14 & #Longs = 8 giving a Monthly profit of $2442
- Your Capital has Grown from $14K to $33K
- The Cum Profit is $19,999
- We have used 2 sig Covered Credit Spreads & WWI triggered Long Calls & Long Puts as the Option Strategies
- Prudent Rule: Margin required for Credit Spreads should never exceed 50% of Capital in Trading Account

- **My Advice to Traders:** ***Be Patient, Let Capital Grow, Don't be Greedy***

Typical Trading Day for Index Options
- **Open Trading Software**
- **Review Promising CCSS or Longs**
- **Obtain Portfolio Quotes & Enter in OpCmdCntr sheet**
- **Evaluate CCSS & Long Positions**
- **Place CCSS and Long Orders on Broker Website if beginning of New Op Mo**
- **Check on Execution of Orders placed on Brokers Website**
- **Make any Protective Moves of Threatened short Call or short Put Positions**
- **Enter End of Day Market Data in Trading Software & Check for WWI Triggers**

Website Aids to Use During Trading Day
- My Yahoo Website, customized to include Your Portfolio real time and also includes real time intraday & 5 day charts to visualize market: http://my.yahoo.com/p/d.html
- DTN.IQ realtime quotes: Subscribe from http://www.dtniq.com/ , to have your private Portfolio established using data my software and easy for you keep maintained
- This Real Time Portfolio can be copied and pasted on OpQte2 sheet which then updates the realtime connections in SelfAdapDTN4 workbook.
- If you are doing currency trading, using my SelfAdapCur workbook
    http://www.mgforex.com/eng/forex-tools/content/forex-rates.htm has real time Currency quotes that can be copied and pasted on the CurCmdCntr sheet of SelfAdapCur.xls program which shows the WWI for each of the Currencies: Euro, Swiss Franc, Yen, and British Pound

- If you are doing Future Option trading using my SelfAdapFutOp workbook, Orion has a free Website for Quotes: http://www.orionfutures.com/ for entering Futures into my software
- The Jon Schiller Program: SelfAdapFutOp has a FutOpCmdCntr sheet for entering the Orion Website quotes which displays the WWI for each of the Futures in the Program
- Note: there's a total monthly charge of about $100 for these valuable Websites to aid your Options & Currency Trading during the day

How to Become a Successful Options and Currency Trader

- Select Strategies with a High Probability of Profit: I use:
1. 2 Sigma OEX Covered Credit Short Spreads (WWI)
2. Welles-Wilder Indicator (WWI) Triggered Long Calls & Long Puts
3. WWI Triggered Buying and Selling Currency Lots
- Learn How to Execute the Strategies doing a Month of Paper Trading using a spread sheet for paper trading such as my SelfAdapDTN4 and SelfAdapCur programs which you may buy from me downloaded as attachments my email to you.
- Open Brokerage Accounts that Have Easy to Use Websites for Trading such **TradeKing** https://www.tradeking.com/ which makes it easy to open CCSS & Condors and Long Calls & Puts. They also have AutoTrade which I use with http://www.disciplined-qqq-trading.com/ for trading QLD & QID
- Develop a Capital Growth Plan that Allows the Loss of One Month per Year, you must be mentally prepared for losses during Option and Currency Trading and use logical trading to make adjustments to threatened spreads.
- Fund your Account with Capital you Don't Need for Your Standard of Living

Dr. Jon Schiller

- Execute your Growth Plan with Patience and take advantage of the Leverage of your Trading Capital for Index Options Trading and Currency Trading

Appendix A: My Options, Futures & Currency Trading Programs
Availability of SelfAdapDTN4, SelfAdapFutOp, SelfAdapCur, and
SelfAdapSigIndicOEX Excel Programs from Author by email Attachment

I did research underlying the basis for these programs while I was living in Spain and have augmented my strategies since returning to California in 2001. I can send these programs and User Manuals in WinWord format to my readers for a small fee of $70 each or $199 for all, as an email attachment. I would attach these as separate files to try to avoid overloading your email servers capacity. The largest size of these files it 6.7+ Megabytes. These are well done programs, to aid your Options & Currency Trading.

I have a monthly update service for $120/year each or $300/year for all packages.

If you should wish to order this package, then send the email order to:

Jon Schiller, Author at email address: jonsch1@verizon.net and I will send you the files immediately.

Then send a check in US$ for the amount of your order made out to my wife at the address below:

Emilie Smyth
701 E. Pine Ave. #118
Lompoc, CA 93436
USA

My Website provides more information about my software and books:

http://www.jonschilleroptions.com/
I have a booger website which also describes my Books
http://wwwjonschblogger.blogspot.com/

Description of My Latest Excel Programs for Options and Currency Trading available from Author by email Attachment:

SelfAdapDTN4.xls for OEX, SPY, QQQQ, SPX, and 14 high-tech
   stock options trading

SelfAdapFutOp.xls for KCWheat, Corn, Soybeans, Coffee, Gold,
   Crude Oil, SPX, 30 Year US Bonds, 10 Year US Notes, &
   Yen Futures Options trading

SelfAdapCur for trading Euro, Swiss Franc, Yen, & UK Pound
   currencies & one hedge

   SelfAdapSigIndicOEX.xls is a bonus program: which has
charts for all the market signal indicators such as MAD4, MAD9-
4, MADC, Stochastics%K-%D, with 4 Input, 3Level Neural
Network to show OEX market Trend.

   I created these new programs after I returned to California
after living 2 decades in Spain. I can send these to my readers for
a small fee of $70 each as an email attachment. I would attach
these as separate files to try to avoid overloading your email
servers capacity. The largest size of these files it 6.7+ Megabytes.
These new programs, utilize all of the *now available internet aids
to Option Trading* not available during the time period I lived in
Spain.

   I am very enthusiastic about currency trading because of
the high leverage to your trading capital. One lot of currencies
which is worth about $100,000 can be bought or sold for a margin
of $1,000. I learned the techniques for currency trading from a
currency expert from Madrid.

   The charts in these Self Adaptive programs are based on
the fact that the WWI can be used as a trigger to buy Long Calls
(WWI<20) or Long Puts (WWI>80). The WWI can also be used as
a trigger for buying or selling a Lot of foreign currency. I have
updated the data so you could use the spread sheets and charts on
the day you receive the attached programs.

Appendix B: Some Current Internet Aids to Options Trading

The Aids Are Used by the Self Adaptive Programs

SelfAdapDTN4 uses two sources of data for aids to options trading:

- DTN.IQ http://www.dtniq.com/ which provides real time quotes which can be entered into the program by copying from Watchlist and pasting in OpQte2. The cost of this portfolio service is about $40/month. I use the portfolio for SelfAdapDTN4 Trading Center sheet uses for keeping real time tracking of your options trading during the trading day.

- CBOE,   website: http://www.cboe.com/DelayedQuote/QuoteTable.aspx?TICKER=OEX provides 15 minute delayed Option Chains quotes for any Index or Stock which has options available. I use these by copying the option chain quotes and then using *paste special – text* to enter into special sheets for each Index and Stock for which the 15 minutes delayed quotes are obtained. These chains quoted include *all* options for all strike prices and all months including for LEAPS. I find these quotes useful when making correctional changes as well as for planning the next month covered credit spreads for OEX or other index or stock you may use.

- My Yahoo provides real time quotes and real time charts for any Stock in your Portfolio or for the Indexes. For example, the website address for the OEX compared to SPX which I find useful for tracking intraday market movements is http://finance.yahoo.com/q/bc?t=1d&s=%5EOEX&l=on&z=m&q=l&c=&c=%5EGSPC   This real time charting service includes historical data and other information useful to trading. It costs about $30/month and is well worth the cost.

- Orion provides quotes for all available Futures and their options. I use this for keeping my SelfAdapFut.xls program updated daily. This program is free and the website is: http://www.orionfutures.com/
- I use MGforex as a real time source for currency data. The real time currency website is: http://www.mgforex.com/eng/forex-tools/content/forex-rates.htm My SelfAdapCur software has a macro initiated by CtrlX for entering the currency data copied from MGforex into my CurCmdCntr sheet which keeps track of real or paper currency trades.

Appendix C: $VIX & XEO, Option Symbols & Greeks

Options on $VIX

The CBOE began trading options on its Volatility Index ($VIX) in the first quarter of 2006. We consider this a major new derivatives product. It provides the first opportunity to trade options on volatility in a listed marketplace. (They have traded over-the-counter, institutionally, for some time.)

The CBOE website had the VIX options chain for Jul options during the last week of the Jul 2008 options month. The Jun options expiration were 18 Jul 2008 The VIX Chart is shown for 5 trading days in November 2007 in Figure C.1 below:

European-style feature, which means that XEO is not subject to the

* Uncertainties involved with possible early exercise. (On the other hand, the OEX® S&P 100 options and most equity options have an American-style exercise feature that allows option owners to exercise at any time up to and including the last trading day before expiration.)

* Unique pricing characteristics. Because of their European-style exercise, some XEO options might be cheaper than their OEX counterparts with American-style exercise.

* P.M. settlement. XEO and OEX options are subject to P.M. settlement, which refers to the use of the closing price of the index on the last trading day (usually the third Friday) as the basis for settlements of exercises and assignments.

* Full-value XEO LEAPS. Investors wishing to manage long-term exposure can use full-value XEO LEAPS®.

* Investment Power and Flexibility. XEO options may allow investors to participate in the price movement of a large segment of the domestic stock market with a single transaction. Bullish, bearish and neutral investors can all use S&P 100 options to implement their individual opinions of the S&P 100 market. XEO options can be used for profit or protection, with opportunities to adjust for changing markets.

Option   Symbols: Reference:
http://www.optionseducation.org/basics/symbols_and_quotes.jsp

Stock Option Naming Conventions & Expiration Month Codes

The Stock Options names are written in the following manner:
SYMBOL MP
Symbol = The Option Root Symbol
M = Expiration Month
P = Strike Price

Example: MSQGN

Microsoft	July Call	$70
MSQ	G	N

Expiration Month Codes

Month	**Call**	**Put**

Expiration Month Codes

Month	Call	Put
January	A	M
February	B	N
March	C	O
April	D	P
May	E	Q
June	F	R
July	G	S
August	H	T
September	I	U
October	J	V
November	K	W
December	L	X

Non-Standard Strike Price Codes

These are general non-standard strike price codes. They can change at the discretion of OPRA without prior notice.

Non-Standard Strike Price Codes

Price	Code
7 ½	U
12 ½	V
17 ½	W
22 ½	X
27 ½	Y
33	Z

Standard Strike Price Codes

Strike Price Codes

Price					Code
5	105	205	305	405	A
10	110	210	310	410	B
15	115	215	315	415	C
20	120	220	320	420	D
25	125	225	325	425	E
30	130	230	330	430	F
35	135	235	335	435	G
40	140	240	340	440	H
45	145	245	345	445	I

Strike Price Codes

Price					Code
50	150	250	350	450	J
55	155	255	355	455	K
60	160	260	360	460	L
65	165	265	365	465	M
70	170	270	370	470	N
75	175	275	375	475	O
80	180	280	380	480	P
85	185	285	385	485	Q
90	190	290	390	490	R
95	195	295	395	495	S
100	200	300	400	500	T

Option Greeks:

Options traders often refer to the delta, gamma, vega, and theta of their option positions, as the "Greeks" The Greeks provide a way to measure the sensitivity of an option's price to quantifiable factors, as defined below.

Delta Δ

The ratio comparing the change in the price of the underlying asset to the corresponding change in the price of a derivative. Sometimes referred to as the "hedge ratio".

For example, with respect to call options, a delta of 0.7 means that for every $1 the underlying stock increases, the call option will increase by $0.70.

Put option deltas, on the other hand, will be negative, because as the underlying security increases, the value of the option will decrease. So a put option with a delta of -0.7 will decrease by $0.70 for every $1 the underlying increases in price.

As an in-the-money call option nears expiration, it will approach a delta of 1.00, and as an in-the-money put option nears expiration, it will approach a delta of -1.00.

Gamma Γ

The rate of change for delta with respect to the underlying asset's price.

Mathematically, gamma is the first derivative of delta and is used when trying to gauge the price of an option relative to the amount it is in or out of the money.

When the option being measured is deep in or out of the money, gamma is small. When the option is near the money, gamma is largest.

Vega ν

The amount that the price of an option changes compared to a 1% change in volatility.

Vega changes when there are large price movements in the underlying asset and vega falls as the option gets closer to maturity. Vega can change even if there is no change in the price of the underlying asset, this would happen if there is a change in expected volatility.

For example, if the vega of an option is -96.94 and if implied volatility were to rise by 1% then the option value would fall by $96.94.

Theta ⊖

What does it Mean?   A measure of the rate of decline in the value of an option due to the passage of time. Theta can also be referred to as the time decay on the value of an option. If everything is held constant, then the option will lose value as time moves closer to the maturity of the option.

Theta is part of the group of measures known as the "Greeks" (other measures include delta, gamma and vega) which are used in options pricing.

Investopedia Says...   For example, if the strike price of an option is $1,150 and theta is 53.80, then in theory the value of the option will drop $53.80 per day.

The measure of theta quantifies the risk that time imposes on options as options are only exercisable for a certain period of time. Time has importance for option traders on a conceptual level more than a practical one, so theta is not often used by traders in formulating the value of an option.

Appendix D: Some Website Options Brokers

One of the most significant changes during the 23 years I have been options trading is the ease of trading that website brokers has enabled. When I was living in Spain and options trading in London, all trades were made by telephone. Now you may make your pick of website options brokers. All of these brokers are dictated by the SEC and the CBOE, so they all have similar trading rules and features. I will not try to pass judgment on which are best, but I do encourage you to research the website brokers available. This can be done easily by using the Google search engine to aid you.

Here are some results of my own Google search:

- Trade King: http://www.tradeking.com/   This is the broker I now use. They have easy to use website with features such as being able to enter Spreads, Double Spreads (Called Condors) and advanced order features such as: Contingent, Trailing Stop, One-Triggers-Other, and One-Cancels-Other.
- Think   or   Swim: http://www.thinkorswim.com/tos/client/index.jsp
- Interactive   Brokers: http://individuals.interactivebrokers.com/en/main.php
- OptionsXpress: http://www.optionsxpress.com/welcome/broker_comparison.aspx?cmpid=gsus21017869
- Lind-Waldock: http://www.lind-waldock.com/platforms/
- OptionsHouse: http://www.optionshouse.com/home/jump/savings.htm?pc=goo

I'm sure you could find other brokers, but I believe a broker from the above list could suit your needs.

Here are some features that The Trade King website provide:

1. Ability to place Spread Orders on OEX, SPY, QQQQ, and other stocks
2. Ability to place Condor Orders
3. Ability to evaluate the % Probability that a Spread Strike Price will finish safe
4. The Advanced Order Features mentioned above: Contingent, Trailing Stop, One-Triggers-Other, and One-Cancels-Other.

More details on the Advanced Order features:

One-Triggers-Other (OTO) With a One-Triggers-Other order, traders can enter an initial order and place a second one that is contingent upon the fill of the first order. With One Triggers Other, clients are actually placing two orders at once. The first is sent to the market immediately, the second is sent to the market only when the first one is filled and it applies to both stock to stock or stock to option trades.

One-Cancels-Other (OCO): With a One-Cancels-Other order traders can enter two orders simultaneously; when one order is filled the other order is automatically cancelled. This feature also works for stock to stock or stock to option trades. For a more on OCO, go to Don Montanaro's blog :
http://bigdog.financialblogs.com/post/blog/_introducingone_cancels_other.html

Trailing Stop: A trailing stop order is an order in which trader enters the stop trigger price is specified in terms of points, or a percentage above or below a security's market price (bid, ask, or last). If the security's price moves in a favorable direction after the order is placed, the stop trigger price will adjust itself automatically and "trail" the market. If the market moves towards the trigger price, the stop trigger will remain constant and the pending order will be sent after the trigger price has been reached.

Stop orders remain "hidden" from the market and competing traders until the stop price is hit.

Contingent: A Contingent order is when the trader places an order with a regular GTC, Market or Limit order that is sent to the market only after a certain contingency is met. The Trader decides the contingency when he place the order with TradeKing. ***The contingency can be either the price of a stock or an option.*** When the price of the stock or the option that the client has set is met, their order will be released to the market place.

Dr. Jon Schiller
US$50

www.ingramcontent.com/pod-product-compliance
Lightning Source LLC
Chambersburg PA
CBHW060529210326
41519CB00014B/3180